The saga continues… 2010-2019 - A Tip of the Hat collection of Idea-rich tips and thoughts from Canadian Ideaman, Bob Hooey

# Introduction

For 22 plus years I wracked my brain to find something informative, funny, provocative, or at least entertaining to share with my readers, clients, and subscribers. We did an **Ideas At Work** newsletter every month for 10 years.

In creating this book (two volumes) I decided to go though those posts and articles and share a few that I felt might be of value to you. Trust you will enjoy what I picked for you.

Excerpts from 22 years of writing and musings from **Canada's IdeaMan, Bob 'Idea Man' Hooey**

*Picture is me getting ready to host our 2013 Global Speakers Summit event.*

We held it in Vancouver, BC. It was called, **The Music, The Magic, and The Message**. Our purpose was to continue supporting our CAPS Foundation as well as help start foundations in some of our other **Global Speakers Federation** member organizations. We were successful on both objectives. This was my final event as a trustee of our CAPS Foundation board where I had served for the previous 5-years. I worked along with my fellow board members to take us from an idea to a functioning foundation able to assist our speakers, should they need help. **A Tip of the Hat to all those who have helped me over the years.**

When this writing project started, I didn't realize how much I had written over the years and ended up splitting the collection into two volumes. 1) **The early years** (1998-2009) and 2) **The saga continues** (2010-2019) and who knows, perhaps there will be further volumes and maybe one final called 'The last years'. ☺

Anyway, I trust you will be able to find something in this smorgasbord of two decades of ponderings. I've compiled them by year and picked some of the better ones. Some ideas, some good news, some travel adventures… all in one place.

## Bob 'Idea Man' Hooey
**Author, speaker, adventurer**

# 2010

## 2010: Something new

*"Today, I will experience something new. I will learn from the world around me: from the words I read, the sounds I hear, the touches I feel, and the faces I see.*

*Even through the course of my daily tasks, I will try to search for a new perspective, lean towards understanding, and make the commonplace a wondrous place to be."* **Susan Polis Schutz**

**Think about the past year...**

- Looking back over the past year, what have you learned, what have you done?
- What is different in your life based on your *'on-the-go'* education and experience path?
- Are you better equipped to lead, love, learn, or serve than you were a year ago?
- What successes have you experienced and who shared in helping you achieve them?
- Is there something that you wanted to do and for some reason didn't get it started or completed?

**Our life is made up of interactive experiences.**

Each April (my personal New Year), I take a short planning break and ask probing questions like these. My life's goal and intent are to live my life to make a leveraged difference in the world. I take time to revisit my dreams and see how I have done building solid foundations for success under those sky condominiums (castles). I also know that what gets measured gets rewarded and can be adjusted for finer focus.

It works well for me and has helped me keep focused along the way to deal with challenges as I sought to successfully learn and enhance my life. If you, like me, have found a missing piece or two in the last year, be of good cheer and resolve to move ahead on it today. Life is too short to live in regret. **Live forward!**

*"It is never too late to be what you might have been."* **George Eliot**
**Here are a few suggestions to help maintain an attitude of constant learning:**

- Take a class at the local college, continuing education, or community center.
- Join Toastmasters and work on becoming a better leader and communicator.
- Explore that hobby you've found intriguing.
- Start a journal, begin a blog, sign up for Facebook, LinkedIn, etc.
- Take up a sport. It's a great way to meet interesting people.
- Explore your own city or town as though you were visiting for the first time.
- Resolve to read selectively and strategically to advance your career. Commit to finding and reading **one book a month** that will serve this quest.

I know when you come home after a long and sometimes challenging day this might not sound like fun to you. However, your energies can be replenished and enhanced when your mind is actively engaged in something that challenges and inspires you.

I challenge you to invest time thinking, reflecting, dreaming, scheming, planning, or just plain working on your future. It will bring dividends beyond your wildest dreams.

Let me leave you with one more thought from **Vincent Arcoleo**:

*"Life can be so hectic, leaving you with little choice but to be swept up in the hustle and bustle that each day brings. Make today special. Slow down for awhile, maybe even stop time... forget your responsibilities and concentrate on your dreams."*

## 2010: What a gift! A gift of giving your attention and time to someone else!

**The Christmas season** has become a rush of *frenzied* activity – shopping and gift wrapping and finally delivering those gifts. Then we collapse, hoping we have chosen something that the recipient will like or at least use.

We often forget the *reason for the season* and the *best gift* is our love, our friendship, and our companionship. When we listen and allow those around us to talk, to be heard, be they young people or older people, we affirm their worth and acknowledge them as people. This is the way we like to be treated and how, I hope, we treat our family and clients.

**When we invest time connecting, listening, and talking with other people we give the best gift of all – ourselves.**

Thanks again for the gift of sharing, of allowing me to come into your email boxes every month. It is a privilege I don't take lightly.

**This year focus on building better, richer relationships. I'll bet you also end up building better careers, businesses, sales results and, of course, friendships and more vibrant relationships with the ones you love.**

## 2010: *"Everyone is born a genius, but the process of living de-geniuses them."* Buckminster Fuller

Too many people today needlessly suffer from comparing themselves to other people and seeing their skills in action tends to make them focus on their own lack of skills. They are quick to sell themselves short or to downplay their own skills or genius. Yes, I said genius.

For at least the last decade I have been challenging people to **unleash their own genius** and apply the creativity inside of them to building and creating a better life, a more productive career, a more profitable or well-run organization. One of the programs I conducted in Vladivostok, Russian Far East was on applied creativity. It was very well received.

I just finished reading a book from the creative mind of **Dr. Wayne W. Dyer** on **The Power of Intention** which touched on this area. I decided to draw from it and whet your appetite. Pick it up and make it a must read and, more importantly, a must apply book before the fall. Wayne quoted **Dr. David Hawkins** from **Power vs. Force**: *"Until one acknowledges the genius within oneself, one will have great difficulty recognizing it in others."*

**You have the power of genius inside of you... and you have the key to unlock it and unleash it in a world that so desperately needs it, and you!**

**Wayne W. Dyer's ten step program** for putting this into reality: "It is my intention to: appreciate and express the genius that I am."

**Step 1:**  Declare yourself to be a genius.

**Step 2:**  Decide to listen more carefully to your inner insights, no matter how small or insignificant you may have previously judged them to be.

**Step 3:**  Take constructive action toward implementing your inner intuitive inclinations.

**Step 4:**   Know that any and all thoughts that you have regarding your own skills, interests, and inclinations are valid.

**Step 5:**   Remind yourself that aligning with spiritual energy is how you will find and convey the genius within you.

**Step 6:**   Practical radical humility.

**Step 7:**   Remove resistance to actualizing your genius.

**Step 8:**   Look for the genius in others.

**Step 9:**   Simplify your life.

**Step 10:** Remain humble while staying in a state of gratitude.

He ends this chapter with a quote from **Ralph Waldo Emerson,** *"To believe in your own thoughts, to believe what is true for you in your private heart of hearts is true for all men (and women) – that is genius."* The above was excerpted from **The Power of Intention** by Dr. Wayne W. Dyer

I have seen people in acts of creation, of genius if you will, who have no idea of their own brilliance... and often, when I point it out, they will downplay their brilliance.

**STOP downplaying your gifts, your skills, and your brilliance.** Shine forth and be a mirror to the world so they too may begin to shine. I realize I am preaching to myself at this point as well.

## 2010: Perceptions

We often think of large multi-store chains as big and impersonal, driven only by market share and profits. This is not always the case. Here is a letter to the Editor that Irene noticed in a local paper shortly after Christmas that made her cry. It brought tears to my eyes too, as well as admiration and inspiration. This story shares a **great example of the true spirit of Christmas**. It also shares a living example of true Customer Service and a winning attitude in retail and business in general. I was inspired!

**Letter to the Editor (Edmonton Sun, Dec. 24th, 2009):** Just had to share!

I called my stepfather last evening from my home in Havelock, Ontario.

Following his move to the St. Thomas Health Center (Edmonton, Alberta) earlier this year most of his possessions, other than the essentials, were discarded. That included the few Christmas decorations he had. I should mention that he is a strapping five-foot-three and 92 years old.

As he wished to decorate his room a bit, he went to a **Zellers in Edmonton** via a cab to get a $10 tree they advertised. The store was a bit much for him and he got lost. When he finally found someone to help, he was informed the trees on special were all gone.

**I am not sure how, but they established how old he is and gave him a more expensive tree along with decorations for the sale price of $10.** Then they proceeded to get him a cab and made sure he was driven back to the right address.

The story seems to lose a bit in print as I had a lump in my throat and a tear in my eye when he told me about how kind the staff was at this store. I have no idea which store it might be, but if the salesclerk sees this note, they will know who they are and realize they too have a **heart 10 sizes too large**.

**Douglas Leary**

**I wonder:**

- What kind of stories are your clients telling about you?
- What kind of stories would you like to have them tell?
- Would your actions mirror the spirit of Christmas and the true spirit of customer service for your clients?

Your conscious actions to provide true customer service create ripples that can enhance your business and increase your longevity regardless of external pressures.


**2010: A birth certificate shows that we were born; a death certificate shows that we died; pictures show that we lived!**

**Relax, and read this slowly.**

**"I believe** – That just because two people argue, it doesn't mean they don't love each other. And just because they don't argue, it doesn't mean they do.

**I believe** – That we don't have to change friends if we understand that friends change.

**I believe** – That no matter how good a friend is, they're going to hurt you or disappoint you every once-in-a-while and you must forgive them for that.

**I believe** – That true friendship continues to grow, even over the longest distance. Same goes for true love.

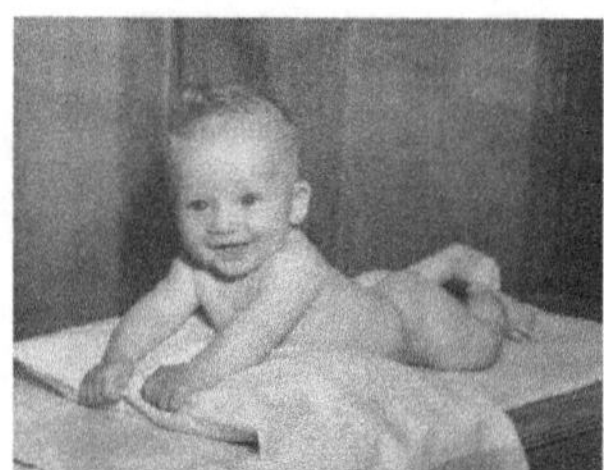

**I believe** – That you can do something in an instant that will give you heartache for life.

*Pic: Me shortly after the start of my un-believable life*

**I believe** – That it's taking me a long time to become the person I want to be.

**I believe** – That you should always leave loved ones with loving words. It may be the last time you see them. (This is so true!)

**I believe** – That you can keep going long after you think you can't.

**I believe** – That we are responsible for what we do, no matter how we feel.

**I believe** – That either you control your attitude, or it controls you.

**I believe** – That heroes are the people who do what must be done when it needs to be done, regardless of the consequences.

**I believe** – That money is a lousy way of keeping score.

**I believe** – That sometimes the people you expect to kick you when you're down will be the ones to help you get back up.

**I believe** – That sometimes when I'm angry I have the right to be angry, but that doesn't give me the right to be cruel.

**I believe** – That maturity has more to do with what types of experiences you've had and what you've learned from them and less to do with how many birthdays you've celebrated.

**I believe** – That it isn't always enough to be forgiven by others. Sometimes you must learn to forgive yourself.

**I believe** – That no matter how bad your heart is broken the world doesn't stop for your grief.

**I believe** – That our background and circumstances may have influenced who we are, but we are responsible for who we become.

**I believe** – Two people can look at the exact same thing and see something totally different.

**I believe** – That your life can be changed in a matter of hours by people who don't even know you.

**I believe** – That even when you think you have no more to give, when a friend cries out to you – you will find the strength to help.

**I believe** – That credentials on the wall do not make you a decent human being.

**I believe** – That the people you care about most in life are taken from you too soon.

**I believe** – That you should send this to all the people that you believe in. I just did.

The happiest people don't necessarily have the best of everything; they just make the best of everything they have. **"The will of God will never take you where the Grace of God will not protect you." Well said!**

**People ask me where I get the ideas for articles, point to ponder and such...** sometimes other people send along pieces that fit. **My catalyst role is to share inspiration and creative challenges with my audiences and readers.**

*This one (above) came from Irene who got it from someone who sent it to her. Not sure who penned this... but it was worth sharing. Enjoy...*

**I believe in you and your potential to move outside of your comfort zone into your winner's zone. You can do it!**


## 2010: DAD... you're still my hero!

With **Fathers' Day** (June 20th) rapidly approaching, many North Americans will be thinking about getting a card or present for that special man in our lives... our fathers. Sadly, for some of us, Fathers' Day is a day of sorrow and remembrance of fathers no longer with us.

*"I remember watching the tears flowing freely down my mom's unbelieving face of grief as we gathered to pay tribute to my dad* **Ronald Howard Hooey** *in February 1999. I watched, as she seemed to shrink before my eyes under the weight of her grief.*

*I listened as person after person got up to share stories of how much my dad had meant to them and how he had impacted their lives.*

**I wondered, did they ever tell my dad of their admiration and love.**

*Dad with my uncle Ralph during WWII*

**"As I got up to share my thoughts and to honor my dad, I was overwhelmed with the loss of the man who had been my hero."**

- **The hero** who had chosen to be my 'DAD' by adopting me those many years ago.
- **The hero** who had modeled love in everything he did, and in how he treated my mom, my sister, and me.
- **The hero** who always seemed to have time for me, despite his own busy schedule; to talk, to challenge, to discipline when I needed it (and I did quite often during my teen years).
- **The hero** who had always been in my corner, believing in me, encouraging me, and loving me regardless of how I was progressing.
- **The hero** who, the night before he passed away on his 82nd birthday, had called me to tell me how much he loved me and how proud he was of me.

I was so glad I'd had the chance to tell him often how much he had meant to me over the years and that the **last words I'd said to him** the night before he passed away were, **"I luv you Pop!"**

My challenge to my fellow children across the globe is not to wait until it is too late. If you love your father, don't wait until Fathers' Day or worse after he cannot hear you. **TELL HIM NOW** and tell him often! **Dad, you are 'still' my hero; and you will be until I join you someday.**

**Note:** My dad passed away on his birthday, Feb 11th, 1999, He would have been 82. I still miss his wisdom, his love, and his warmth. He was my best cheerleader and champion. He was very special to me, and I would like to remind you that Fathers' Day is not the only day to express your love. **Tell them often**. My mom followed him a short 6 months later. I still miss them both!

# 2010: Duke's Creed

*"In Hawai'i we greet friends, loved ones or strangers*
*with Aloha, which means with love.*
*Aloha is key word to the universal spirit of real*
*hospitality, which makes Hawai'i renowned as the world's*
*center of understanding and fellowship.*

*Try meeting or leaving people with Aloha.*
*You'll be surprised by their reaction.*
*I believe it and it's is my creed.*

*Aloha to you."*
**Duke Paoa Kahanamoku**

On our  recent *adventure* to Australia, I mentioned our side trip to Hawaii where we had the *un-expected* privilege of walking down the Waikiki beach, shopping, and finally, as the sunset filled the sky, sharing a meal with **Bob and Rauna May** at **Duke's Restaurant & Barefoot Bar** on the beach, off Kalakaua Avenue.

This *un-scheduled* side trip, due to a medical emergency on our flight, was Irene's 1st taste of the Hawaiian magic and my 20th *official* trip to the islands. Been there a few more times than that... I only count the times I get out of the international holding area for a tour or check in somewhere.

I have enjoyed every single trip to the islands and this day was no different, other than the pleasure of sharing it with Irene. We had a great time exploring together and flew on to Sydney, Australia about midnight later that day with a touch of Aloha spirit in our lives.

Perhaps we will get there again next January for a few weeks of sun and fun and a bit of writing along the way. Perhaps I can write a few of our **Ideas @ Work** issues adjacent to one of the beaches...hmmmm.

**Duke Paoa Kahanamoku** was an amazing man who in his later years became Honolulu's official greeter and Hawaii's Ambassador of Goodwill & Aloha. He is best known for his exploits in the sport of surfing and helped catapult that sport into the spotlight around the world. But there is more to him than just one of the sports he loved, and at which excelled. **Duke Paoa Kahinu Mokoe Hulikohola Kahanamoku** was born into an old Hawaiian family and was one of the last full-blooded Hawaiians. His grandfather was a Hawaiian high chief. His father was a policeman.

**With the world's eyes most recently on BC and the 2010 winter Olympics, I thought I would share some interesting background on the Duke.** You may not know that he was an Olympian for more than 20 years. He won his 1st gold at 21, as well as a silver medal swimming in the 1912 Olympic games in Stockholm; he won 2 more gold medals in the 1920 Antwerp Olympics; he won a silver medal in the 1924 Paris Olympics; and, finally, at 42, he won a bronze medal at the 1932 Los Angeles Olympics.

He also swam in exhibitions in 1918 to raise money for the 1st World War. He was inducted into the Swimming Hall of Fame in 1965; the Surfing Hall of Fame in 1966; and posthumously inducted into the US Olympic Hall of Fame in 1984. In his spare time (1922-30) he played parts in 28 movies while he lived part time in LA. He served the people of the City and County of Honolulu as their Sheriff (1934-59) and was elected 13 times. (Like father, like son.)

He has statues honoring his excellence in swimming and surfing, as well as his role as the Ambassador of Aloha in California, Australia, France, Hawaii and elsewhere. **Not bad for a beach boy who grew up with the ocean as his playground and spent hours doing what he loved most – swimming, canoeing, surfing, and body surfing.**

**Doing what you love** can lead you to creating an amazing legacy that will outlive you and continue to touch people you've never even met. My first Aloha experience happened after Duke had passed away. I still remember it with fondness.

- Why not live your life with enthusiasm and embrace each day as an adventure?
- Why not meet each person with Aloha in your heart and your actions?
- Why not be an Ambassador of Aloha in your community and your career?

**You'll be glad you did and so will your family, your friends, your colleagues, your clients, and potential friends you encounter along the way.**

## 2010: Vincent van Gogh 1853 - 1890
### During his career he only sold 'one' painting.

"**Van Gogh's** finest works were produced in less than three years in a technique that grew more and more impassioned in brushstroke, in symbolic and intense color, in surface tension, and in the movement and vibration of form and line.

Van Gogh's inimitable fusion of form and content is powerful; dramatic, lyrically rhythmic, imaginative, and emotional, for the artist was completely absorbed in the effort to explain either his struggle against madness or his comprehension of the spiritual essence of man and nature."

*I toured the Van Gogh Museum in March while in Holland to speak at the **PSA Holland** convention in Noordwijk which is not too far from Amsterdam. My wife Irene has been 'introducing' me to museums on our trips. Van Gogh was a tortured talent whose artistic excellence was not appreciated until well after his death. That did not detour him from expressing himself and capturing his vision on canvas during his brief and conflicted life.*

"Vincent van Gogh, for whom color was the chief symbol of expression, was born in Groot-Zundert, Holland. The son of a pastor, brought up in a religious and cultured atmosphere, Vincent was highly emotional and lacked self-confidence."

"Between 1860 and 1880, when he finally decided to become an artist, van Gogh had had two unsuitable and unhappy romances. He worked unsuccessfully as a clerk in a bookstore, an art salesman, and unsuccessfully as a preacher in Belgium. He remained in Belgium to study art, determined to give happiness by creating beauty."

"In 1886 he went to Paris to join his brother Théo, the manager of Goupil's gallery. In Paris, van Gogh studied with Cormon, inevitably met Pissarro, Monet, and Gauguin, and began to lighten his very dark palette and to paint in the short brushstrokes of the Impressionists.

"His *nervous* temperament made him a difficult companion and night-long discussions combined with painting all day undermined his health. Van Gogh then began to alternate between fits of madness and *lucidity* and was sent to the asylum in Saint-Remy for treatment.  In May of 1890, he seemed much better and went to live in Auvers-sur-Oise under the watchful eye of Dr. Gachet. Two months later he was dead, having shot himself 'for the good of all'."

**Walking through the museum** where millions have visited, it is hard to imagine *labouring* a lifetime without seeing any positive results, as well as struggling to keep your sanity. I was amazed at the richness, variety, and the vastness of his body of work.

Van Gogh saw the world differently than his counterparts and countrymen.

**He painted with passion and abandonment and created a vast collection of art for those remain to view and ponder.**

- What do you do with passion and abandonment?
- What do you do without regard of acclaim or recognition?
- What can you accomplish in the world when you follow your passion and leave the results to the historians?
- When will you unleash that passion?

*Portions of this note were adapted from a shortened version of Van Gogh's bio.*


## 2010: Anything to declare...?

How often have you heard these words as you stand or sit in line to re-enter Canada after a vacation or business trip? How often have you been scratching your head wondering if you remembered everything, or added it up correctly?

As a professional speaker, success coach, and trainer, I have the privilege of traveling North America and occasionally other countries to share my **Ideas At Work!** My work has allowed me to visit and work in 34 countries on 4 continents so far. This year I have been fortunate to visit Honolulu, Hawaii; Australia (Sydney, Perth, Geraldton, Kalbarri, Noosa Head, and Brisbane); Amsterdam; Detroit, Mi; Mexico; Seoul, Korea; Valdivostok, Eastern Russia; and Orlando, Florida in addition to traveling across Canada.

This month I will be in Phoenix for CAMP NSA and December will see me flying to Montreal for our 14th annual CAPS convention. (*Update 2019: 61 countries on 6 continents, so far, and more to come in 2020.*)

Despite the *romantic* notion of world travel and the privilege to meet people from around the globe, being on the road is not always fun. Late flights, rushed food, not enough sleep, missed connections, and varying conditions for food, service, and variable accommodation can take their toll on your body and your spirit. **I wouldn't miss it for anything – I love what I do! Some trips are even more special as Irene along for the adventure.**

I have to admit, there are times when I've flown nearly 24 hours and had a delay or two enroute that I really want to answer the question, **"Anything to declare...?" with a simple, tired, "Yes, I'm glad to be home and I'm glad to be a Canadian."** How about you?

## 2010: Seven success ideas you can build on!

If we are serious about offering value-added service and meeting the changing needs of our customers, we need to explore some different avenues in helping them solve or resolve their problems. Here are **seven areas** that successful businesses have used in their efforts to assist them. See if some of these lend themselves to your career or business and build on it!

### Showroom or in-store seminars

If your product or service lends itself to being more effectively used by different applications, holding an in-house session is a great idea. How can you adapt or change your situation to be able to offer this service to your potential customers? I used these activities to enhance my career as a successful kitchen designer.

### In-house, client newsletter or e-zine

Keeping in touch and sharing information on how to better use your products or services or what's happening in your industry is a great way to serve. With some of the new software programs, this is increasingly easier to accomplish. I'd suggest doing this 2-to-4 times a year at first, so you don't promise what you can't deliver. Keep it simple and conversational. Keep the focus on "WIIFM" – what's in it for me! Write it from their perspective, if you would truly serve them. It can even be done as an e-letter and sent via the Internet. When will you start? What will you call it?

### Send stories to local media

Become a source of information to your community by taking the risk of sending items of interest to their readers to the media. Keeping people informed about newsworthy developments is a customer service activity. How can you do this in your area? Being quoted or having your articles published can lead to some very productive responses. I was hired to speak for **OK Tire** in Cancun after the lady who was planning the event read one of my articles and decided I was a great fit for her event – then she called to engage me. (*Gee, February in Cancun. Who would have thought?*)

### Write a booklet, workbook, book, or e-book

If you have built a solid reputation or a depth of experience in your field, perhaps you can add value to your service or business by taking the time to write a few thoughts. It doesn't have to be a work of art, just valuable and easily read.

I wrote **"How to Remodel Your Kitchen and Stay Married!"** when I was designing kitchens 15 plus years back. It was a very effective tool! Since I moved into the realm of speaking, coaching, and mentoring I have been able to write and create a wide range of business, sales, leadership, and career success publications. Visit: **www.SuccessPublications.ca**

We've published 4 **Pocket Wisdom** books on Sales, Leadership, Creativity, and Presentation Skills. We plan to publish at least a dozen over the next few years.

### Mall shows or home shows

Another opportunity to provide a needed service to potential customers. It's a bit of work, but it will pay off in the long run. Does your firm or product lend itself to this type of instruction and marketing? Check out opportunities in your area to better serve your customers, by sharing your knowledge and exhibiting what you provide to the market. Is there a mall show in your area that you can enter?

How about a display at a local bank or other location? My **"How to Remodel your kitchen and stay married"** lead to an offer to headline the BC Home Show on my own **Kitchen Idea Stage**. It worked wonders for my exposure and my business. Another area would be to set up a display at local networking and business or professional association events. We do that with Toastmasters.

### Continuing education or guest lecturer

This is how I started and eventually this outpouring of training as a professional kitchen designer allowed me to teach fellow designers and potential customers alike.

Later, we expanded areas of instruction into the areas of time management, creativity and problem solving, and, of course, Customer Service.

I've been a fulltime speaker, trainer, and consultant now for over 15 years (2010); a National charter member of the Canadian Association of Professional Speakers; and a member of the National Speakers Association. **It all started in night school.** What is it you know that would be teachable and provide solid value to potential customers? What is stopping you from taking this step?

### Become a media source

Contact your local media and let them know you'd be willing to act as a source if something comes up within your area of expertise. Often, they are looking for local or national responses to breaking stories. If they know you and your expertise, you might be called on to respond or comment as an industry 'expert.' What can you be an 'expert' on? Make a commitment to let them know!

Visit our **'Creative Collection of Wisdom' Articles** web page for information on how to become known as the expert. **www.ideaman.net/articles.html**

## 2010: Each Life A Legacy

**Our life is a portrait of who we are – autograph your life with style!**

Whether we realize it or not, our life leaves a legacy. That legacy can have positive or negative ripples – the choice is ours. People we know, work or live with will have a lasting impression based on their experience with us. Why is it, that we wait until they are gone to acknowledge the important people in our lives? Life is a choice.

- **Why not leave a legacy that has contributed in a positive way?**

Once we understand that we leave a legacy behind, we can make a conscious choice to make sure it is a positive one. We can choose to invest our time, resources, and energy in helping those organizations that create lasting value and in the lives of those we love and respect. You can start now!

My parents left us in 1999. They left a big hole in the lives of my sister and myself. More importantly, they left a legacy of love and commitment to family and community that has been ingrained and lives on in us. I work to ensure their legacy is enhanced by what is chosen to do with my life and vocation. I dedicate every book written, including this one, to honor them.

- **Acknowledging the accomplishments and contributions of those around us!**

Over the years I've learned that people all too often die unacknowledged and unappreciated. This is one of the biggest losses in our rich culture and legacy as a nation. We have people who have made an impact in our lives; who have made a difference to, and they don't know – because we never told them! Resolve to tell people now and tell them often how important they are in your life and where they have made a difference. It can be the most valuable gift you can give. I work to encourage as many people as I can while I go through my life. My gift!

- **Investing in the lives of others can be our best legacy!**

I've often heard, **"You can't take it with you!"** Interesting thought! In one sense it is true. When we pass away, we leave everything we once held important behind. Someone said, "I've yet to see a hearse pulling a U-Haul trailer." If we take true leadership with our time and resources, we can invest them in the people we want to help now, and in those who might be joining us one day.

Think of all the people who have invested in your life and your success. Some may have passed away. However, their investment in you is still paying dividends as you continue to grow and pass on what they taught.

- **Realize the impact you have and 'choose' to make it a dynamic one!**

We make an impact on the lives of others each day and in each encounter we have. We have an impact on strangers and on people who we may not even know. Like the ripples on a lake that bounce off each other, we have an impact, and we change the patterns of those we connect with, as they have an impact on us.

One of the most decisive and productive decisions I made was to undertake to make a difference in my life; **to leave a positive legacy** behind me. A legacy of empowered and encouraged people, audiences, readers, family, and friends who knew I loved and cared enough to give them my very best. **People who know I believed in them** and prayed for their success and success in life. To making sure my words, written and verbal were based in truth, delivered in love, and focused on the positive opportunities in life.

Lord willing, I have quite a few more productive years ahead of me. I still have book ideas to birth, countries I want to visit (**www.havemouthwilltravel.com**), and friends around the world I have not met, as yet.

But, regardless of the time allowed, I pray that when I go, I leave a legacy as rich as those of my parents **Ron and Marge Hooey**. I would be blessed indeed if I was able to leave that kind of legacy behind. (*this is me pictured with them back in California*)

Interesting how the pics changed over the years. New stories, new adventures, and of course new lessons too. I'm pleased to share some of them with you in this book.

# 2010: CAPS Foundation event in Montreal

*Les, Nabil, Tony, Bear, and Bob celebrating a successful CAPS Foundation fundraiser*

I have been privileged to serve on the board of directors for the **CAPS Foundation** and in part my role is to create and work the CAPS Foundation evenings. This one in Montreal was especially amazing. About 10:10pm I got to go back on stage to announce that we had breached the $100,000 goal to become a functioning foundation. **We reached $103,892. (Update 2019**: I would serve on the board until the end of 2013 and we reached over $250,000.)

**What you think about you often bring about!**
Perhaps you have heard something like this and wondered if it is true for you? I have found, for me, that when I keep something as top-of-mind I tend to work harder in my approach to making it happen. That is one of the reasons

I still use a **print Day-Timer** in addition to my on-line calendar. I find when I write it down, I don't usually have to go back and look at it – it stays in my mind and comes out in on-going my words, thoughts, and actions.

**What do you want to accomplish? Write it down!**

# 2011

## 2011: Coffee inspiration

My wife gave me a couple of coffee mugs for our place in the country last Christmas. I just drank from one of them and paused for a moment to ponder its blended, idea-rich words of wisdom.

**"Behind every success is effort...
behind every effort is passion...
behind every passion...
is someone with the courage to try."**

**And on the inside lip: "GO For It!"
Hmmmm...**

Spring is 'officially' here and I'm hoping to see some 'solid' evidence of that soon. Hopefully the snow will continue to *melt slowly* so we don't flood. This has been a looooong winter for me. Fortunately, we had the week in Cuba at the beginning of February to break it. But it has still been a long one. I am not fond of the cold weather, even less now that I don't take to the ski hills.

**Spring is a time of new ideas and possibilities. Farmers start getting their equipment ready to plant again.** You and I can give our minds and spirits a check up so we can go forth and plant new innovative ideas that will yield amazing results when we cultivate and nurture them over the next few months.

Some of us have had some soul searching during this winter, perhaps even wondering if we were on the right path. That is a normal thing to go through from time to time. That is also a time to touch deep into our passion and suck up our courage to try again.

- **This time, we will make it work;**
- **This time, it will be different;**
- **This time, we will overcome and move on to succeed.**

**Go for it!**

# 2011: What is holding you back?

*"Until one is committed, there is hesitancy, the chance to draw back. Concerning all acts of initiative (and creation) there is one elementary truth, the ignorance of which kills countless ideas and splendid plans: that the moment one definitely commits oneself, then Providence moves too. All sorts of things occur to help one that would otherwise never have occurred. A whole stream of events issues from the decision, raising in one's favor all matters of unforeseen incidents and meetings and material assistance, which no man could have dreamt would have come his way."*
**W. H. Murray (The Scottish Himalayan Expedition)**

**The only way to successfully climb a mountain is to start; to take that first step.**

Yes, it is important to make sure you have a plan, that you've taken care to ensure you have competent guides and a team to make sure your climb is successful. It is important to train yourself and to make sure you are in shape for the challenge ahead.

Somewhere along the line, you must choose to make that first step and then, once committed, continue to make all the steps necessary to reach the summit safely and successfully. Planning and thinking about the climb are important, but you must begin.

Often you will find the actual climb to be more challenging than you could have imagined. I remember (one summer about 35 years back) hiking, what would be considered a small height, up a 4500-foot vertical peak in the BC interior. I went along with the encouragement of 3 of my friends who were in *much* better shape and more experienced than myself. I thought if they can do it so can I.

I practiced walking around my apartment with my 40-pound pack and took long walks around the city where I lived to 'get in shape', and at last I thought I was ready. Boy, was I mistaken. That 40-pound pack would soon feel like 400 and my legs would make me cry out in pain.

We started off very early and the 1st part of our journey went very well. In fact, we found ourselves where we had planned to stop the 1st night just after lunch. This was the gentle part of the trip! ☺ They decided to push on to the summit that same day. Being a 'guy,' I choose to follow despite my already sore body.

**It was excruciating!**

I remember the last couple of hours staggering 50 or 100 feet at a time and then slumping to catch my breath or leaning against a rock or scrub tree. Then I would take a deep breath, shift my pack, and stagger some more.

When at last, I reached the summit... it was truly amazing. We were above the cloud line and looking down saw other peaks appearing like islands in the clouds.

We cooked dinner on the summit. I have to admit it tasted better than anything I had ever eaten. The next day, I stayed at the camp to let my body heal while they went off in search of something else to hike. I enjoyed the solitude of the day and the vision of still being above the clouds.

I reflected on my not fully understanding what I was preparing for in taking on this arduous quest. I also marveled that I had successfully climbed this peak and reflected that I had done it one agonizing step at a time.

*Bob enjoying dinner above the clouds*

**"Until one is committed, there is hesitancy, the chance to draw back."**

What is holding you back from making your dreams a reality? What is holding you back from starting? When will you take the first step to climb your personal mountain?

## 2011: "Friends are worth the distance!"

I used these words in a Facebook posting to refer to our recent trip to Vancouver with two small detours to visit friends. Someone commented on it and it got me thinking.

Irene and I travel during the year, more often to warmer climates but usually do a road trip to BC each summer.

Irene and I just came back from a trip to Langley to see her aunt who is battling cancer. We had such a great time with **Aunt Eva;** you'd never know she was doing chemo and dealing with a short timeline.

Her attitude was so positive. She had decided to return home and live as normally as she could for whatever time remains to her. We hope that will be a long-time but realize it may not.

While we were making plans, we heard from our friends **Wayne and Brenda** who live on Wood Lake and Irene's long-time work friend, **Charlene** and her husband **Randy**, who had just retired to Castlegar last month. Both invited us to visit and we said yes.

**Irene was able to change things at work** so we could leave on the Thursday morning and we were able to spend most of the weekend with **Wayne and Brenda Cotton.** Wayne is a very brilliant man and I've had the privilege of his friendship and consul for many years. When I was first relocated to Alberta and still teaching in Vancouver, BC, I would detour to his area on my way home so we could spend part of the evening chatting and laughing. His wife, Brenda made me feel welcome when I would visit. I looked forward to my visits with them. When Irene and I became a couple, they welcomed her with open arms.

This trip we were able to enjoy time with them on their floaties, shopping, and Wayne and I took a trip to Vernon for an un-believable classic car street show. Some amazing cars: boy would I love to go car shopping there one year!

We even had movie night on their deck. What a blessing they are in our lives.

**Charlene** worked with Irene at the Alberta Research Council for close to 30 years and they have a very close friendship. When I entered the scene Charlene and Randy welcomed me as a friend. Many dinners and a few outings were spent laughing and chatting. I think Charlene misses everyone at work and was overjoyed that we would detour down and back to Castlegar to visit. So was Irene, I think she missed Charlene too.

We had a chance to see their new home, did the art walk downtown, and went for a visit to the beach along the Columbia River behind the dam. Even though it was a short visit, it was great to see them.

As I said on my FB posting, **"Friends are worth the distance!"** When you have good friends, you don't mind a detour or two to see them. In fact, you look forward to doing so because you enjoy the privilege of their friendship.

Our jaunt to BC took us about 3500 km, about 1100 more than just driving direct and back. Those extra km were worth the distance because the friends we visited were worth the distance. How far are you willing to go for your friends? Who would go the distance for you?

## 2011: Family memories

**Christine Bigoray** and our newest addition to the family. We love having Kelly and Christine as a part of our extended family and love watching **Alexa** and **Isabell** growing up.

They have added so much fun to our lives and in a way allow us to be grand parents or aunts and uncles.

**Kelly** has taken on keeping our vehicles in good running order and is an amazing mechanic and friend. I often go over on the weekends to watch him repairing someone's car or truck just so I can spend some time with him. We are truly blessed to have them in our lives.

## 2011: Christmas is a time for reflection, recreation, and re-connection.

Christmas is also a time to spend with family, friends, and colleagues as well as a time to share gifts. As I reflect on the year just winding down, I am reminded of some of the some of the more valuable gifts I have enjoyed.

**The gift of trust** with my clients across the globe;

**The gift of friendship** and support from my colleagues, friends and family;

The continued gift of a patient, loving woman (Irene) to share it with; **The gift of being surprised** in Toronto with **The Spirit of CAPS** award for 2011; and, most importantly, the gift of *each of you* being a part of my life and my business.

To each of you I wish the very best of Christmas wishes. May your hearts be overflowing with joy and gratitude for those who care. May you be comforted for those you have lost. May you and your families be blessed and enjoy your time together. May you and you co-workers or employees see this next year be a prosperous one for all.


## 2011: Surprise

**Have you ever been totally surprised at something?** Surprised that you had done something that people noticed? Or talked about? Me too!

My trip to Toronto started with a hectic rush to make airline connections so I could arrive in time to help my friend **Wayne Lee** with the CAPS Foundation fundraising event we'd worked on for about 6 months. It was an amazing success with us raising **$35,083.00** over the evening. This was a great highlight for the year and for the work everyone put into this evening.

The next day we had our CAPS President's ball and awards banquet where I saw my friend **Dave Rodwell** go on stage as President of CAPS Edmonton when it was announced that we'd earned the top award for adding new Chapter members. Bravo!

Then, minutes later fellow CAPS executive members **Dave Rodwell** and **Dune Nguyen** were on stage as a part of a Strategic Partnerships committee given a Presidential award. Following that, we had the Hall of Fame and I saw my friend **Colleen Francis** inducted. Wow!

Then, at the end of the meeting, **2011 CAPS President Ravi Tangri** came on stage to present the last award of the evening. **The Spirit of CAPS** is the highest award we present within the Canadian Association of Professional Speakers.

We do so to **'recognize one member's contribution to excellence in the speaking profession and their commitment to the ideals and values of the Canadian Association of Professional Speakers.'**

I was listening as President Ravi Tangri started introducing this person... when he mentioned this person was the **1st Canadian to attend CAMP NSA,** I realized he was talking about me. I couldn't believe what I was hearing. I was shocked and deeply touched at the same time. As I wiped the tears from my eyes on the way to the stage to accept this amazing award, I wondered what I would say.

Evidently, what I said was pretty good based on the positive comments on it. I have contacted the company who was filming the evening to see if I can get a copy.

**Here it is, give it a listen:**
**https://youtu.be/E4RpjfcPTO8**

I shared this award with the hundreds of people who said yes when I asked for help. Even though I was singled out for this honor, I did not achieve it alone.

We don't work for the honors and the recognition, but it sure is nice to find out someone noticed and appreciated our efforts. I think that spurs us on to find other ways to serve. It does me!

## 2011: *"Great minds have purpose, others have wishes."* Washington Irving

I know I am probably 'writing to the choir' here, but perhaps we need to be reminded that **our 'purpose' is the driving force in our life, our career, and in our leadership within our community.** I run into too many people who, as you listen to their language, prove the truth of Washington Irving's sage observation. **They are living their lives on wishes, *not* living on purpose.**

**Living on purpose** is like having a good compass to guide you and help you make the course corrections needed to keep you focused, motivated, and confidently moving forward. It helps you stay true to your values and enhances your character despite any challenges and detours you encounter.

- What is the purpose by which you guide your life, your relationships, as well as your organization or career?

- How do you ensure your purpose remains foremost in your mind and evident in your decisions and actions?
- Has it changed in the last year? If so, how will it drive your actions this year?

**Robert K. Greenleaf**, founder of the modern Servant leadership movement wrote, *"Purpose and laughter are the twins that must not separate. Each is empty without the other."*

Part of my life purpose is to laugh, to love, and to lead by example. In fact, on our Ideaman.net site I have my own personalized **'Robert's Rules'** of which the first is **'The Rule of Fun!'** I find that having fun and allowing myself to see the humor in each situation makes it easier for me to stay true to my life purpose. Having fun allows me to better serve my audiences, readers and clients. I also look forward to some beach time as reflection, recharging, and recreation this year. Visit: **www.ideaman.net/Rules.html**

## 2011: Confidence about Credibility

*"No one gets taken seriously in this world unless he or she has credibility. Not credibility about brilliant ideas or heroic deeds, but credibility about daily habits and performance."*

**A successful and sustainable career or business is built on established credibility.**

Your clients, employers, and co-workers want to be able to trust and rely on you to do what you say you'll do – when you say you'll do it. As you read through these **4 credibility factors** (following), pause, and ask:

- How would you rate yourself and your co-workers or staff in these areas?
- Are there areas in which you see improvement needed?

**Here are the four basic ways in which we establish our credibility:**

### Showing up on time

Time is the most valuable commodity we have. It is precious in that it is finite and cannot be banked or saved - it must be used wisely.

**When you devalue my time - you devalue me!** Show me I can count on you to be there, and I begin to trust you.

### Doing what you say

Follow-through and doing what you say is rare. Often, based on experience, we expect to be disillusioned, to be lied to and disappointed. When we aren't, we are pleasantly surprised and your credibility soars. **Under promise and over deliver!**

### Finishing what you start

What a nice surprise, when we discover that you finish what you start. What a difference this makes in the corporate field. This sets you apart from your competition. Resolve to start and complete what you commit to doing if you want to build a successful business or career.

### Saying please and thank you

Common courtesy is not that common. As individuals, we are often treated with a lack of civility or respect. Show appreciation for people and their willingness to deal with you. This will serve you well and win loyalty.

**These simple points may seem self-evident. Failure to observe them is the biggest cause of loss of credibility in our relationships.**

In an increasingly competitive global economy, your clients want to feel special. They want to be able to trust you.

- **More so, with increasing competition, credibility is a career survival and business-building tool.**

- How would you rate yourself and your company in this area?

- **How would you change what you're doing now to ensure they get that opportunity?**

## 2011: Little hinges swing big doors

As I travel North America and recently, the globe, I share a few basic ideas or messages with my audiences. I tell them, **"Once people fully understand the 'Why?' (purpose) the 'How's?' (processes or procedures) tend to take care of themselves."** Simple little idea, isn't it?

These little things seem to slip the grasp of many of our North American leaders. We tend to complicate things.

**W. Clement Stone**, who built a billion-dollar sales organization in the depths of the great depression (early 1900's), shared a key quote that has been close to my own growth and success. He worked with **Napoleon Hill,** who authored, 'Think and Grow Rich', published Success Magazine, and hired and mentored **Og Mandino**, who authored motivational classic, **The Greatest Salesman in the World**. Stone wrote: **"Little hinges swing big doors."**

Successful, entrepreneurial leaders constantly search and are open to finding the next 'slight edge', the next profitable idea, or 'little hinge.' I do too!

*"It's the little things that make the big things possible. Only close attention to the fine details of any operation makes the operation first class,"* offered **J. Willard Marriott**

- What little hinges have you applied in your life to open big doors or opportunities?
- What hinges have you used to leverage your skills and expertise to better your career, company, or community?
- What is next for you?

## 2011: What is your GAP?

If you are like me:

- Perhaps there is a **GAP** between what you say and what you do?
- Perhaps there is a **GAP** between what you believe and what is true?
- Perhaps there is a **GAP** between your dreams and your reality?
- Perhaps there is a **GAP** between your intentions and your actions?

That is, for the most part, a normal situation in each of our lives. Each of us needs to work on reducing the GAPS in our lives or in filling them if we are truly committed to growing and becoming more productive in our lives and careers.

**For example, people do see and often judge the GAPS in our lives.** When what we do is far removed from what we say, our credibility suffers. When what we believe and what we see (true) are separated, we can undermine our confidence.

When our actions fall far short of our intentions or our dreams are so much more than our reality, we can find ourselves a bit frustrated, disappointed, and disillusioned.

At times the GAPS can seem to be insurmountable or impassable. And, for a time they can be. Here are a few ideas that might help you close the GAPS in your life.

**Refocus your beliefs, dreams, and intentions.** Are they really aligned with who you are and who you want to become? Are they worth the investment in time, money, and effort to bring into reality?

**Resolve to make changes.** Changes in your efforts, your investment, and your commitments. Changes in what you say and do. Changes in what you share with others.

Perhaps, like me, you need to learn to be a bit less vocal about what you are going to do and just do it. When I first joined Toastmasters (1991) telling everyone I had the grand intentions to be an international keynote motivational speaker (and that really was my goal). However, my skills were very 'basic' at that point and the statements seemed to be unrealistic and perhaps egotistical. Hmm. Somewhere during that first year, I stopped talking about what I was going to do and started digging in on my presentations and I began to slowly improve.

As I did, people came along to encourage and to guide me with solid, useable tips and techniques that helped me hone my skills. It took a few years, but eventually I moved into the realm of professional speaking and again dug in... and again saw some improvement. And then, one day I realized I was living my dream... and guess what? It still needed work. Smile!

**Resolve to allow people into your lives** who can help fill the GAPS or perhaps provide bridges to allow you to cross them. I have been fortunate to have quite a few people; fellow Toastmasters, fellow CAPS and NSA Members who chose to invest in my life and leadership.

My wife, **Irene Gaudet** was one of the best GAP fillers in my life. She has helped and supported me, and I am a better man, a better husband, a better speaker and coach because of her.

They stood in the GAP for me and helped me in ways I will never be able to repay.

I find myself still learning, still looking to close the GAPS in my life. But I am still moving towards my dreams, intentions, and actions. **Where are the GAPS in your life?** What are you committed to do to fill them or at least make them smaller? Life is full of challenges but is made better when you keep focused on the goals and take steps in the right direction.

## 2011: May was a momentous month in many ways…

- Oprah had her last show completing a successful 25-year run.
- My cousin and her husband escaped the Slave Lake fire with what they could throw into their 5th wheel and had their home burn to the ground.
- My sister and her husband sold their house in St. Albert.
- My 98-yr old neighbor Steve had his house demolished.

**Life can be funny at times as we grow through 'passing' points** and see things we have loved left in the dust of history.

*Bob and his buddy Steve at grandson Stephen Bigoray's wedding*

Steve is now living in a Veterans home and has his good days. His home had been vacant since last September when he had his heart attack. He hadn't been able to come back, and it was becoming a liability. His son arranged to have it demolished as it was too far gone to repair. Sad to see it go.

It was the place where he and his wife brought up their two sons after the war and visited with friends (including me) and family over the years. His grandson **Kelly Bigoray** lives across the alley with his wife Christine and Steve's great granddaughter Alexa. Steve's family home had a good run. Perhaps, in the future, one of the boys will build something there and the cycle will continue. For now, it is sad to see the vacant lot where Steve once lived.

**Trudie and Doug Moon** were fortunate to get out with their 5$^{th}$ wheel and what they could pack. Their house was burned to the ground, while their daughter's house was spared. My cousin and her husband will likely rebuild and move back to Slave Lake… it has been their home for many years, and they love the area. I'm sure they will make design changes in their new home to reflect their status as grandparents vs. parents when they originally moved in.

**Patti and Jerry Cholak** (my sister and her husband) sold their place in St. Albert and are moving into a Sherwood Park condo for a year while they both wait for surgeries. Then they will decide where they will retire. They are downsizing and lots of 'stuff' is being given away or sold so the remainder will fit in their new home. Irene and I will have to do this in a couple of years when we combine our two houses.

I watched a part of the last Oprah celebration show and was inspired. Not so much about all the guests or stars she helped to launch; not that she has become an amazing success and now has her own TV network; and not that she was on for 25 years. Each of these are worthy accomplishments.

**Her greatest accomplishment was the education she paid for and helped provide for 64,688 young people around the world.** Now that is truly amazing.

In life, we have points at which we have a choice to let go and continue to grow. Letting go comes in various means; sometimes we chose it, and sometimes it choses us. **In each case, we can make the choice on how we handle it and whether we stop or whether we move on.** Keep moving…


## 2011: Are you taking advantage of all your opportunities to be happy?

*"I don't know what your destiny will be, but one thing I do know, the only ones among you who will be really happy are those who have sought and found how to serve."* **Albert Schweitzer**

**Are you happy in your career or business? Does it show?**

Many of us miss amazing opportunities to bring a little joy into the lives of our clients, and through that ourselves, when we forget why we are in business. I tell my audiences **_"The main purpose of business is to make the lives of our clients better, at a profit."_** Profit is not a bad word – it is the life blood that enables us to be there when they need us again in the future.

I had the privilege of sharing these and other thoughts for **Edmonton's Business Link** a few years back. We broke new ground as we videocast that presentation to 17 other centres across Alberta and Saskatchewan. When we are too focused on the daily challenges of dealing with conflicting demands, customer quirks, and the hectic pace in which we live and do business, it is easy to forget.

We lose the joy and zeal we had when we first started. This is a downward spiral making life more difficult and our relationships less satisfying. This spiral can be _easily_ halted and reversed. It's a matter of perspective and choice!

Our success in business and life is built on long-term mutually productive relationships. Those relationships are enhanced and enriched when we reach out and touch people. A few years ago, I had the opportunity to visit with my friend **Eric Chester**, CSP when he was presenting here in Edmonton. Eric is the leading authority on dealing with **Generation Why?** He has a book out _"Getting them to give a damm"_.

**_"There is a great paradox in reaching out to touch someone – and that is, the more you reach out to others, the more you will be touched yourself. Joy and happiness in great measure are waiting for us if we will reach just a little further,"_** writes **Joan Rawlusyk**.

**My challenge for you** is to make a _conscious effort_ to reach out and touch the people who personally contact with your life and your business. Be open to sharing joy and happiness in whatever you do.

**_"Let us be grateful to the people who make us happy; they are the charming gardeners who make our souls blossom."_** **Marcel Proust**

I have been blessed by many amazing gardeners who have helped my soul to blossom… to each of you, I say THANKS!

**2011: This is dedicated to my buddy Steve Bigoray who passed away last Friday (July) at 98.**

*This picture was taken on Steve's 97th birthday.*

As many of you may know, he was my next-door neighbor until he had a stroke last September and was not able to live by himself anymore. He was much more than a neighbor. He was my friend and he allowed me to be a part of his extended family.

We spent a lot of time together over the past almost eleven years.

I will miss his kind words, his gentle heart and his crusty exterior. I loved him!

He made me laugh and he added so much to my life as well as Irene's. He was the grandfather I never had, and I so enjoyed my time with him.

His funeral was yesterday afternoon, and I had the rare privilege of saying a few words at the request of his family. I also had the privilege of being one of his pall bearers in escorting him to his final resting place. The Legion sent an honor guard to be a part of his funeral. They added a respectful touch to their fallen comrade that was truly inspiring. Kelly, Christine, and Alexa hosted a friends and family gathering on the new deck we were working on over the past few days. It was a great time to gather, tell stories, and share our respects for Steve Bigoray.

## 2011: What is important to you?

With all the news of floods, earthquakes, and other disasters around the world and the devastation they've caused in people lives **I wonder what is important to you and me?**

Thousands have lost their homes, their livelihoods, and even members of their family. In some areas many will be losing their jobs. In Cuba there will be 500,000 people who will be laid off in the tourism sector this May.

Here in North America there are many who are still out of work or under-employed, struggling to make ends meet. And, yet I hear many who are, in my opinion, blessed and spoiled who are complaining and whining about *trivial* things. Sad!

Makes me give my head a shake at times. I know what it is to go through rough patches and to be so close to loosing it all. I also know what it is like to be living in a life of blessing and abundance. Have to say, I prefer the abundance.

**The real secret is how we look at what we are dealing with... good and bad.**

- **Are we grateful for what we have?**
- **Are we grateful for the challenges in our life?**
- **Do we see them as important in making us who we are?**

**On the other side of the coin:** Irene's cousin **Ann Hurley** is overjoyed her son Jamie came through his open-heart surgery. My speaker friend **Catherine Armstrong** can hardly wait to fly to Australia to meet her grandbaby for the first time. As I write, this my wife who loves me is working at her computer not 4 feet from me, and our furry kids are laying in their respective baskets... so life is good!

Irene and I were in Cuba early last month for her birthday and came away with an increased appreciation for what we have and what is important to us. Our new friends in Cuba taught us that you can have virtually nothing and still enjoy life if that is important to you.

**What is important to you?**
**Who is important in your life?**
**What do you want to accomplish that is important as a legacy?**

## 2011: Sales tips

If your career or success depends on your ability to persuade an audience or buyer, these five tips on delivering **effective sales as well as business presentations** will help you understand how to structure your presentation for maximum effect. I've applied these tips as I travel the world speaking and inspiring a wide range of audiences. You can too:

- **Dress appropriately:** Dress for Success – not excess! Make a point of understanding the dress code for the group or situation.

One suggestion would be to always be **a bit better dressed** than your average client or the best dressed person in attendance.

- **Use short sentences, simple phrases:** Make it easy for your client or your audience to gain acceptance and understanding of your concepts. Don't assume that they are fully literate – keep in mind most of the daily newspapers *(read by many executives)* are written to grade 6-to-8 levels.

- **Avoid humor unless appropriate or relevant:** Effective use of humor can be a great bridge. However, you can blow yourself out of the running by using something that offends a client or someone in the audience. They may not even tell you, but they won't buy from you or deal with you.

- **Distribute any handouts at end of your presentation:** This idea applies to any use of handouts or brochures. Unless you need to have them refer to them, use them as a tool or write something in them during your presentation – leave them for the end. People tend to read what you've given them instead of listening to you. This is especially important in sales situations.

- **Don't bluff. If you don't know, find out!** Your credibility is a fragile thing in the business arena. Do your homework so you have the basics at your fingertips. Don't try to wing it or fake it when asked a question outside that parameter. **Make sure you understand the question** and make a specific commitment to find out and get back to them. Then do so!

**Business leaders** today, as well as your clients and audiences, are busy. It is critical that you be clear and concise to win and keep their attention. Unless you know them personally, start strong, present value, and conclude with impact.


## 2011: Point to Ponder

As I write this, I am sitting at our home in Mundare, AB. I'm getting ready to drive over to meet with a client to work out details and schedules for a two day (April weekend) strategic planning and visioning retreat for their town councillors and senior staff. We'll be talking about what is important for them in moving forward to becoming a more viable and sustainable community.

I have facilitated similar meetings for a few other groups over the past few years. Each has its own challenges.

**Facilitation in this kind of situation can be a challenge.**

1) Getting people to talk and to share their input and ideas in a public forum,
2) Controlling those who like to talk a lot.
3) Keeping everyone focused and energized as we work for a common goal.

As I write this, I am drinking coffee from a mug that has this little inscription:

## "NEVER LET YOUR MEMORIES BE GREATER THAN YOUR DREAMS"

**How cool is that!** A part of the visioning process leading up to strategic planning is getting people to dream, to see in their minds what could be... not what is or what used to be.

When I first started speaking, I remember sitting in a little fish and chips shop in Adelaide, Australia talking with my new friend **Peter J. Daniels**. Along with some advice and tips for sustained success in this business, Peter challenged me to dream bigger and to stretch myself. Good advice.

I challenge people to **dream big dreams** and then work to build solid foundations for success under those dreams. I challenge myself on this path as well. Some of our greatest advancements in history began as a dream. Many of those became realities when someone was diligent enough to begin crafting a plan to build them or make them work. Many of the joys and successes I have come to enjoy started as dreams… dreams built on!

**What are your dreams?** Are they greater than your memories or are you living in the 'back in the old days I did...'?

Do you still remember them?
Are you still working on them?

**Dust them off,** polish them, hone them, refocus them, and then get working to make them a reality. Dreams along with strategic planning and action become the success stories that inspire others to dream too.

## 2011: Mental Vitamins and brain exercises

The mind works best when challenged with a daily routine of creative thinking, just like an exercise program designed to condition the body's muscles. The late **Earl Nightingale**, noted self-help expert, devised a very simple method that requires **three things:**

- **An open mind**
- **A pencil or pen**
- **A pad of paper or something to write on.**

The system or method he devised works as well today as it did when he introduced it to his readers and listeners. Here is my recollection of his system, as I practice it.

1. **Give your subconscious a pressing problem** to digest and gnaw on just before you go to sleep. Spend 20-30 minutes thinking about a challenge, problem, or opportunity you are dealing with currently. When you lay down forget about it. While you sleep your subconscious mind, the source of most breakthrough ideas, will be mulling it over and thinking about it from various perspectives and sides.

2. **Wake up an hour before anyone else**. Find a comfortable place to sit, get a coffee or juice, a pad of paper, and a pencil or pen. This can be my biggest challenge as I often am creative late at night. The key here is to pick a time when you will not be distracted or disturbed.

3. **Relax and let the ideas flow**. Write everything down as the ideas occur, no matter how wild, far out, or seemingly impractical they seem. Don't stop to edit or judge these ideas, just capture or record them. This is a **solo brainstorming** session. Capture and collect – analyse and judge later. Let your mind do a mental dump onto paper into a form you can do something with later.

This simple brainstorming method worked like a charm for Earl, on a regular basis. It produced some profitable, outstanding ideas, which he later launched successfully.

According to Earl, the key is the subconscious mind, which acts like a gigantic *warehouse for ideas* and thoughts, floating around just below our conscious mind awareness. Insights or hunches are ideas, which simply bubbled up from the vast reservoir of our subconscious mind.

Studying or feeding your mind a problem or outlining an opportunity just before you go to sleep, is like stuffing your subconscious mind. This feeds your powerful brain new fresh material to play with and from which to work.

Try this simple form of personal brainstorming, you might inspire yourself with the wisdom you draw from your subconscious mind. Once you have generated ideas, simply transfer to your computer for further research, refining, or editing.

# 2011: New beginnings

*"Every new beginning comes from some other beginning's end."*
Seneca

*"It is always a great time to begin again.*
*It is never too late to start over.*
*It is always good policy to renew and move on.*
*It is always a good thing to renew your faith in yourself.*
*It is good to consider who believes in you and your growth.*
*It is seldom a bad thing to stop and reflect on the lessons you've learned.*
*It is a great day to make new plans, new friends, and to renew old ones.*
*It is always a great time to begin again."*
© 2011 **Bob 'Idea Man' Hooey**

**Life has its challenges** and I've enjoyed a few along the path. No doubt, I will enjoy more as I continue working **in** and walking **on** this journey of mine.

In life and in business we often need to begin again. Sometimes that means leaving something behind; something that no longer fits or suits us; something that is no longer in tune with the world around us.

**What do you need to let go of?** What is holding you back from your new beginning, your new journey, or your new challenge? It takes courage to begin again and to let go of those things, activities, beliefs and sometimes people who are holding you back. Are you a person of courage? What will you begin?

Hard to believe all the years that have passed.... **72 issues with 72 thought provoking points to ponder**... wow that is motivational in itself! I went back and re-read some of them and was amazed at how relevant many of them are for us now.  We **(Ideas At Work!)** are committed to serving you, to challenging you, and to engaging you to seek your best results; to move from your comfort zone into the winner's zone; and to believing (sometimes in spite of the challenges before you) that you can grow, learn, and be successful.

*"It is always a great time to begin again!"*
**Bob 'Idea Man' Hooey,** *Older, and perhaps a bit wiser, than my last beginning.*

I told someone recently who asked how I was doing, ***"My wife loves me and everything else is a bonus."*** Puts it in perspective for me. That was a new beginning that has brought joy, love, and a sense of togetherness to my life. She keeps me focused and working strategically.

# 2011: What is your 'NEXT' Million Dollar Idea?

*"Today, creativity must go beyond mere idea generation; the light bulb that goes on over the head of the talented person. It must become an ongoing process, not just momentary and isolated epiphanies. Creativity is also a process that is linked to how knowledge is managed, because it is inherently defined by quantum leaps in understanding that lead to the realization of value."* John Kao

Have you ever seen something and thought, **"Hey, I thought of that first!"** Then, mentally kicked yourself because you never did anything about it? Me too!

**Join the 'Million Dollar Idea 'LOST' Club.**

I was working in a Seattle youth ministry, back in 1970, and while sitting around with another Canadian, came up with the idea of a **drive through oil change** business. We figured there might be a market for something faster than making an appointment and waiting at a dealership. I even went so far as to draft up a simple floor plan with a drive over pit; like what I 'now' see when I get my car serviced. But we never acted on it!

I went on to what I was doing and simply forgot about it. My friend went home and acted on the idea, one of the first of its kind, which grew into a large chain across Canada. Now, every time I drive in to get my oil changed, I am reminded that **it is taking action on our ideas that makes them profitable – Ideas At Work!**

**Why do we do this?** Is there a cure to help us? Can we move out of this club and into the **"I acted on My Million Dollar Idea Club?"** Well, the answer is simply, yes! Our newest Pocket Wisdom book is designed to do just that. Using a very simple format, I want to challenge you to create or capture an 'idea-a-week' that will help to enhance your personal or leadership performance as well as your organization.

This newest Pocket Wisdom is going to the printer today! I finally reformatted it from its current size to fit into our Pocket Wisdom series.

The key in what I shared about is not just having the idea but acting on the idea. **Ideas At Work!** which happens to be what we called our company.

**Why not join the 'Million Dollar Acted On It' club instead?**

My challenge for you is to take stock of the ideas you've got rambling around or written in journals and evaluate them from the perspective of **DO or Not Do!** Very often we are sitting on a potentially profitable idea or have been letting it gather mental dust while we are engaged in other less important activities.

Someone once told me that, **"the critical, productive activities are often at the mercy of the menial, less important ones."** Too often we live our life in the shadow of what **might have been** instead of boldly stepping into the ring.

**Does every idea pan out and make a million dollars?** Nope, some fail miserably. Some create some nice streams of income, like our Secret Selling Tips. But you will never know until you make the commitment to **ACT** and to move **AHEAD** on implementing them.

I've had some great ideas along the way. Some have been very productive. Some have added love and a partner I enjoy spending time with. Some have been detours which have created lessons I can use in the future. I have not always jumped, but I have had the courage to step out and work on them. You can too!

Like my friend, **Kelly Falardeau**, who just published her 2nd book this year, **"Self Esteem Doesn't Come in a Bottle!"** It hit the Amazon best seller lists last week. I'll bet she'd say you can do it too. I have had the privilege of contributing to both of her books and stand in awe of what she is doing with her life and her career in this industry.

Like my friend **Charmaine Hammond**, also a best-selling author, whose book **"On Toby's Terms"** is to be made into a movie. I'll bet she'd say you can do it too!

So, what is stopping you from reaching out, dusting off a dream or two, and moving ahead to make it a reality?

*"Empty pockets never held anyone back. Only empty heads and empty hearts can do that!"* **Norman Vincent Peale**

I had the privilege of working with Norman and meeting him and his lovely wife Ruth, when my partner, **Larry Darling** *(deceased)* and I hired him and other speakers to do a one-day motivational program. I do remember this (at that time mid 60's) little old man shuffling out on the stage at the Jubilee Auditorium and holding the crowd mesmerized for over an hour. He was amazing in person. I was hooked!

Back stage, I said to myself,
**"Some day I want to do that!"**

Well, it took 22 years before I acted on that idea; but it is one that has allowed me to literally travel the globe sharing ideas of hope and help with tens of thousands.

If you've had a dream that just won't go away, perhaps now is the time to take it out, dust it off, and do something about it.

**Don't let your dreams die within you.**

*This picture with some of our Rotaract students was captured when I was speaking in* **Vladivostok, Far Eastern Russia in** *June 2010.*

## 2011: Dedicated to our 'Clients', who may choose, at times, to be our 'Customers'

As you dip into our **'Make Me Feel Special!'** you might notice we have used the word 'client' sprinkled throughout this publication on ***Idea-rich strategies for enhanced customer service;*** in some cases, using both 'client/customer'. This is a *deliberate* choice in our vocabulary and a *foundational* change in mindset we feel necessary to help you enhance your chances of attracting and retaining customers who will become your biggest fans and champions (i.e. clients).

Business success (retail, service-based, or even direct buyer connections) is built on establishing mutually profitable relationships; relationships where you make the customer (client) feel special.

**When you *'Make ME Feel Special!'* you enhance your chances of converting 'me' from a one-time customer to a long-term raving client and champion.** *(visit www.SuccessPublications.ca to get yours)*

*Client vs. Customer: Aren't they really the same thing?*

**Webster's defines these seemingly interchangeable words**
- **Customer:** one that purchases a 'commodity' or service
- **Client:** one that is 'under-the-protection' of another; a person who engages the professional advice or services of another

Ever wondered why the top performing business owners and sales superstars sell so much better and make so much more money than their counterparts? Plus, they seem to do it much easier, too. **Their secret** is in how they 'visualize' and more effectively approach everyone, which results in higher levels of success with their prospective clients.

- **They 'see' clients** vs. customers walk into their locations and act accordingly.
- **They 'see' clients** when they pick up the phone or walk into an office or boardroom.
- **They 'see' clients** when there is a concern or something that needs to be fixed or replaced. They act with a long-term view.
- **They 'see' clients** who gladly become raving fans and champions for them.

Take a moment and reflect on the underlying *'differences'* in the meanings of these two words. The way a person who does business with you can be approached and treated will directly impact your results. In the past, you may have referred to them as customers. **Please think of them as long-term clients!**


## 2011: Winter arrived in style over night this past Friday.

As we slept warm in our bed last Friday this strange white flaky stuff fell from the sky, blanketing the cars, the roads, the flower beds, the decks, and even the pond at which I ponder.

**We awoke Saturday to 3 inches of wet snow** at our place in the country. A novel experience – the 1st time it happens each year.

Not one I enjoy as it is a glimpse of future snowfalls and shoveling to come. Ok, this year I am almost ready as I shoveled at least 10 tonnes of gravel for the parking pad – which is now covered in white. But I am still not looking forward to moving it around until it starts melting next spring. Just being honest. I am looking forward a couple of years to our retirement when we will be able to slip away to a warmer climate for at least a couple of the winter months.

**Now before you think I have gone entirely negative, I do have a point to this ponder.**

We had a marvelous day at CAPS Edmonton with one of our best attended programs this year, a very talented MC (**Michelle Devlin**) and a very smart presenter (**Jane Atkinson**). I left encouraged and inspired to tackle a few of my own challenges to changing what I do in the evolving industry.

When we drove home to our place in Mundare, guess what? It had snowed there too! I was not looking forward to cleaning the driveway and pulled up on the side of it so I could shovel. This is where this takes a positive turn just in case you were wondering.

As we got out of the car, a young girl about 8 or at the most 10 was walking across the street. Her first words were, "Do you live here? **Would you like your driveway shoveled?"** Her rosy cheeks radiated her willingness, with just a hint of hesitation.  **I asked, "How much?" Her reply, "5 bucks." My immediate reply, "Go for it!"**

She proceeded to shovel. We proceeded to clean out the car. We asked her if she wanted to use our shovel as it was a bit bigger. She said no. Interestingly, her shovel was taller than she was. She worked at it and got most of the snow off in a short while.

I asked her how many jobs she had done that day. Her reply, **"You're the first. The rest were either not home or didn't want it done."** She was an eager beaver. Sad that her entrepreneurial offer was not recognized or accepted. Their loss!

When she finished her cheeks were even rosier. I paid her and slipped her a tip, just because; and she headed off in search of another client. Usually when I finish shoveling the driveway and the parking pads, I am a tad tired and warm, perhaps cold too. I had a distinct warm feeling when she finished. I was encouraged and inspired at the same time.

She reminded me of what it was like to set out to do something, to deal with rejection, and to continue searching. She reminded me what it was like to have youthful confidence and enthusiasm in approaching a challenge or a job.
She reminded me of the importance of continuing to ask and to ask again. We quit when the next ask might be the one that gets us to 'YES'.

The next time you find yourself up against a challenge; perhaps hearing 'NO' a few more times than you'd like, remember this young teacher of mine. If she can do it, so can I – so can you! **Keep working, keep shoveling, and keep asking.**

I will attempt to keep her in mind next time I am cleaning off the driveways. I live in hope that she will remember us and come back. Please come back little girl, it is still snowing. And it will continue. She could learn the next lesson of repeat business... smile!

# 2011: "I DO!" … and I still do!

Two words made all the difference. Whoever said, "Talk is cheap!" did not speak the truth.

*Bob and Irene following their wedding ceremony in Las Vegas Oct. 4th, 2008*

3 years ago (Oct 4th, 2008), **I married my best friend**. Irene and I were married in Las Vegas, NV by a local pastor. When the Pastor asked me the traditional question, "Do you take Irene to be your …" I tearfully said, **"I DO!"** and I did! Thankfully she said, "I DO!" too. All she said when we decided to get married in Vegas was, "No drive through and no Elvis."

When I asked her on the cruise to Los Angeles, "Would you like to get married?" She simply said, **"YES!"** and that one word started the amazing journey we are on now.

**My life changed, for the better! Irene has enriched my life in too many ways to outline here.**

Life can be a long and lonely road and having someone you like and love along makes the journey more fun and more satisfying. Irene and I love and like each other and support each other.

We travel well together and enjoy each others' company. We have divergent interests and politics and that helps to keep us fresh and vibrant. I am so grateful and blessed to have Irene in my life.

**I got a bonus family too, her daughter Amanda and son Alex.**

Once you make the commitment things fall in place. Two simple words, "**I DO!**" or **"I WILL!"** can make a major difference if you are a person who lives up to your words.

- **Your words** can lead the way to creating a path where there is no path.
- **Your words** can lead to creating a team from a divergent group of individuals coming together for a common goal or good.
- **Your words** can inspire others to step up and move past their comfort zones.
- **Your words** can set you on a journey of personal leadership and action on ideas and dreams long dormant.
- **Your words** can bring hope and help to others who are struggling; people who can learn and build from your lessons.
- **Your words** can express the love, affection, and appreciation so missing in our lives. People are dying for words that touch their souls. You can speak them!

*I am now working on the creation of our CAPS Edmonton leadership team as I will be their leader and President for 2012. Each of them said "I will" (in some form or other) when I asked them to help me and the chapter. What are you willing to say when challenged to step up, to make a difference, to move ahead? Will you say, I DO?*

## 2011: 12 Key Strategies for 'Bringing Out the Best in People'

*I originally wrote this leadership piece many years ago and have shared its wisdom around the world, in person and in print.*

*I deliberately revisited it at this time as I am moving into a new leadership role. I will share this issue with the new team members and challenge them to challenge me to practice what I preach.*

**Alan Loy McGinnis** wrote a book back in the last century about bringing out the best in people. It was well-received and gained exposure and acceptance among progressive leaders at that time.

Over the years, I've had the chance to reflect on what Alan outlined. As I wrote this piece, I had his 12 rules sitting on my wall above my desk as a visual reminder of how important they are in leading and coaching the people I work with across

North America, and more recently around the globe. If you are committed to be an effective leader or manager, perhaps they should be sitting somewhere close, so they are not far from your mind's eye. They provide the foundation for effective management, leadership success, and leveraged teamwork.

Apply them well to equip and motivate your team to succeed. I include them, along with my own reflective thoughts, for your inspiration and illumination.

### Expect the best from the people you lead

See them performing at their best. People will rise or fall to the level of our expectations. See them as they could be, not as they are! Don't limit them by expecting less than their best.

### Make a thorough study of the other person's needs

Each person on your team is an individual with specific skills, talents, strengths, weaknesses, needs, and dreams. Taking time to know them makes it easier to lead and direct them for mutual success. It allows you as manager or leader to help them succeed in their respective role.

### Establish high standards for excellence

Leaders fail when they accept mediocre results or fail to set challenging standards. People will amaze you when you set the bar higher and lead by example. Don't be afraid to challenge your team to live up to and surpass achievable goals and standards.

### Create an environment where failure is not fatal

Mistakes are a natural part of life and taking risks means occasionally you fall short. If your team feels supported and encouraged, they will take risks and move past their comfort zone into the winners' zone.
Help them learn from the lessons of any mistakes or miss-steps and move ahead with energy to face the next challenge.

*This point, when shared during a presentation in Tehran, Iran got me into a nervous conversation with one of the clerics in the audience. He 'took' me aside, following my presentation to talk about it. But that is another story.*

### If they are going anywhere near where you want to go, climb on other people's bandwagons

Sometimes you need to be honest and realize that people are not always going the same direction or share the same values that you live. In that case, let them go and stay your own course. If they are going where you want the team to be, let them lead and be supportive. Be courageous enough to realize that you can follow your own path. Others who share your values will follow.

### Employ models to encourage success

This goes to the heart of leadership by example. Make sure this is modeled in your own management life and in the lives of those you promote, train, and delegate to succeed.

### Recognize and applaud achievement

People do not work simply for money or position. Each has his or her own needs. One of those needs, deep inside each of us, is the need to feel appreciated, informed, and important to the team. As a leader or manager, the most effective thing we can do is to recognize achievement and effort from those we lead and to share and publicly applaud their achievements.

### Employ a mixture of positive and negative reinforcement

We understand it is a good thing to provide praise and positive reinforcement in our team members' efforts. This affirms their actions and encourages them to move ahead. It is also necessary at times to apply the opposite tack when one of them is doing something detrimental in the fulfillment or follow through of their role. Letting them know what is 'not' acceptable is also part of a leader's role. We can do it nicely and in kindness but do it we must if they are to grow and maximize their potential. Amazingly enough, people appreciate knowing their boundaries.

### Appeal sparingly to the competitive urge

Each of us has a natural competitive edge. If used wisely, competition can be a great tool to higher achievement. It has its 'dark' side in allowing divisive actions and attitudes to creep into a team environment. Focus on the team accomplishment and mutual win. Encourage each to compete for higher standards and personal skill development.

### Place a premium on collaboration.

This is where **team – 'works',** and where effective managers and leaders learn to pull people from diverse backgrounds, agendas, and experiences into an effective unit. Brainstorming is one way of effective collaboration allowing each to build and draw on the brainpower of one another. It is a great way to energize your team and draw from their creativity to drive innovation and growth.

**Build into the group an allowance for storms.**

It is not always smooth sailing as a leader or in managing team efforts. Storms, difficulties, challenges, detours, and disasters can strike when you least expect them. As a leader you need to build in allowances for these speed bumps in your team's progress and have some plans in place to cover each potential challenge. Sometimes you need to step in, give clear directions, and help them weather the storm.

**Take steps to keep your own motivation high.**

You are 'on' as a leader all the time. This means people will be looking at you and taking their cue from you. It also means you need to keep your personal motivation high and maintain a positive outward attitude. This means you may need to find a trusted advisor or fellow manager who can discuss your challenges in private. Letting your negative feelings show can be devastating to your team. They look to you as being confident, clear in focus, and consistent in action and follow through. Don't disappoint them.

**Learn to apply these management rules of the leadership road to smooth out your path and make it easier for those who follow you to walk in it.**

### 2011: *"Surround yourself with those who believe in you and will help you achieve your goals."* Lisa Marie Yost

When you are struggling, and that happens to each of us, remember to apply the wisdom in this quote. As someone once said, *"the best time to dig a well is before you are thirsty."*

Building a valued support network is a worthy activity if your desire is long-term success and growth. These valued friends, coaches, cheerleaders, and champions will help you weather the storms and detours life puts in your way. Invest time along the way building your network and remember it works both ways. You have the responsibility of being there for them as well.

Life can be challenging at times. Careers and businesses go through dips and detours. Make sure to keep focused on your goals and dreams. Having a supportive network will help in this regard. It has for me; more often than I can count. I am so blessed with the amazing people in my life. My wife, my friends and colleagues, and my clients who invite me into their organizations.

*"If people offer their help and wisdom as you go through life, accept it gratefully. You can learn much from those who have gone before you."*
**Edmund O'Neill**


**2011:** My friend **Kelly Falardeau** is just finishing her second book, **"Self Esteem *doesn't* Come in a Bottle"** She kindly included my contribution in her amazing project: **Here it is…**

Dear Kelly:

How do you 'really' see yourself? How do you value 'You'? How do you determine your own worth?

**Self-esteem is a term used in psychology to reflect a person's overall evaluation or appraisal of his or her own worth.** (Wikipedia) Like many of you, I struggled with these issues for many years, from my childhood well into my adult life.

Still do for very short times. There were times I wondered if I would ever amount to anything or accomplish anything of value. Then somewhere along the way things changed in how I valued myself and how I saw 'ME'.

Somewhere along the way I stopped worrying about what others thought and minimized how I compared to others or even to that 'ideal' picture of myself. I have worked diligently to close the gaps between my visualization of myself and where I really am at any given time. I realize, I have room for improvement and strive to do so.

I am learning to stop and savour the wins (even small ones) along the way. I am learning to graciously accept and evaluate the opinions and observations of others, whether positive or constructive.
I am learning to allow myself to make a mistake or two along the way and to leverage those mistakes into greater accomplishments.

**Here are a few quick ideas to help you create and maintain a healthy self esteem:**

1. **Celebrate your achievements** or wins, however small. Create a scrapbook (print or online) or a wall of fame where you display them. Then, revisit them from time to time. I did this with my hallway in my country place by providing a place for the plaques, awards, and designations earned. When I am assailed by self-doubt, I look at them and re-affirm I have accomplished some amazing things and I can do it again.

2. **Create a warm fuzzy file** where you store the nice things, the compliments, and the positive reinforcement people have given you. As a writer and speaker, I get notes and emails from people who appreciate what I have done. I put them in my warm fuzzy file and re-read them when needed.

3. What do you do to **feed your self esteem**? In addition to the above, what books (like this one) what CDs, Videos, or DVDs do you view? If you feed your self esteem, you will grow stronger. Please remember to give yourself lots of love and positive self talk to help build a healthier self-image.

Self-esteem is a **build-it-yourself** project. I am blessed to have a wife who loves me, a career that challenges me, friends and colleagues who enjoy me, and audiences and readers who appreciate what I say.

**As I see it... Bob 'Idea Man' Hooey**

**Theodore Roosevelt** said it best: ***"The best executive is the one who has sense enough to pick good men (or women) to do what he wants done and self-restraint to keep from meddling with them while they do it."***

This just might be your biggest leadership challenge. (It has been mine on occasion!) Part of your *larger* role as a leader is equipping those you lead to succeed. This means giving them opportunities to fail or succeed without your *'constant'* supervision. Make sure you pick good people, give them good direction and instruction and then, give them room to find their own unique way of handing it.

**You just might learn something new, and they will often amaze you.**

## 2011: *"I got troubles!" Steve Bigoray*

As many of you know I lost my 98-yr old buddy Steve on July 15th, 2011. He had been a delightful part of my life since I moved out to Egremont from BC back in 2000. He and I had so much fun, just talking and hanging out. He loved Irene when she joined the family and would ask how she was if she wasn't out here. **One of the gifts he gave me was his family as part of mine.**

Every so often I would pick up the phone and hear these words above.

I would put on my coat and boots (winter) or just head out the door to see what his 'troubles' were.

Sometimes they were minor, like a blown fuse or the TV not working. Sometimes it was something more serious like the satellite dish out of alignment or his car not working, and we would have to wait until Kelly (his grandson) came home from work. Most of the time it was a small thing that, to a man in his 90's, were challenging; but to a younger man (me) not so. I was pleased to help him and to do what I could for him. I learned a few lessons too. He was a great guy!

### 1) **Ask for help**.
Steve was a very independent man, but he learned that he needed help and he learned to ask for it. One of the biggest lessons I've learned in leadership is to ask for help and advice. I am going to be asking for lots of help as I take on the leadership of my CAPS Edmonton Chapter.

### 2) **Accept the help you ask for!**
Enough said. You don't always have to heed the advice, but you can acknowledge those who offer it. If you ask for help, be gracious and allow them to do so. This honors them and helps build a solid relationship.

### 3) **Return the favor.**
Where you can, return the favor. When you can't, pass it forward. I remember Steve's son Ron wanted to build a bigger garage. He and Kelly had kept my car serviced and running and I appreciated their help and friendship. **Kelly Bigoray** now helps keep our cars in good running order. I remember telling Ron, *"I don't know much about cars, but I can swing a hammer."* Ron and I would frame walls and when Kelly and Stephen came home, we would put them up. Each day I look across the lot and see the garage that we built together.

### 4) **Keep in mind your troubles may be smaller than you think.**
Often, to us, each trouble can seem to be insurmountable. Sharing your concerns can make a major difference in bringing them into perspective. Steve and I talked about all sorts of things and often just talking helped me see things in a different light. I have this kind of relationship with my wife, Irene, and it helps me in many ways to be able to openly talk about the various challenges in my life. She is a pretty smart lady and I love her for that wisdom.

### 5) **Take responsibility for your self.**
This can be a tough one, but when we take personal leadership and responsibility we begin to move ahead. Steve eventually decided he didn't want to drive which made many of us relieved. When he had to go to pay bills, he would suggest we take his car, and would then hand me his keys.

**Note:** Just had a bar-b-que on Monday and Steve's grandson Kelly, Christine, and now, one-year old Alexa attended. We were joking that I would now be able to call them when I had 'troubles' of my own in 25 years or so.

## 2011: What drives you?

*"Only a clear definition of the mission and purpose of the business makes possible clear and realistic objectives. It is the foundation for priorities, strategies, plans, and work assignments. It is the starting point for the design of managerial jobs and, above all, for the design of managerial structures."* **Peter Drucker**

- What is driving you and your team?
- What is your defined purpose and strategic mission as an organization?
- What is your defined purpose and strategic mission as an individual?
- What are you providing for your prospective clients or customers?
- What are you doing to engage and motivate your team?
- What are you doing to equip yourself and your team to grow and win?

Funny how some non-structured time in the sun with a good book allows your mind to wander and wonder. Amazing how the warmth and sea air can stimulate your imagination and your ability to dream. The end of each quarter is a good time to pause and reflect on how you and/or your team are doing.

Remember those goals you set late last year or early this year? Hmm. I found myself rethinking *'what I do'* and *'why I do it'* on a February working trip to Cancun. (*pictured here*) I had a wonderful time addressing the dealer/owners of a major Canadian National Tire Chain.

They were very receptive and open to challenge their own experiences and to revisit *'why'* and *'what'* they were doing. This, I believe, is the beginning of building strong, long-term foundations for profitable growth and success under any organization. Know what drives you help build long-term profitable client relationships.

From personal experience, having a *'strongly defined'*, visual image of your purpose and a strategic mission of what you do will keep you focused. It will also keep you fired up and excited about your business and career. It will help you ride the tough times and challenges that come with everyday life and modern-day business.

My challenge for you is to take a minute... ok, 15 minutes, and take a serious look at what you are doing. **Ask yourself,**

- Why are you doing it?
- What real value do you bring to your industry, market, and clients?
- What are you willing to change to make it better, more attractive, and value-added to your team and your client/customers?

***Make ME Feel Special! Idea-rich customer service strategies*** *by Bob 'Idea Man' Hooey has been updated and re-written for 2020* **www.SuccessPublications.ca**


## 2011: I love what I do and the amazing folks I share it with...

*Bob (Canada), Gustav (South Africa), Phillip (USA) and Paul (Netherlands) at the 10th annual PSA Holland convention in 2010*

Whenever I can I work to build in time to present at one of our Global Speakers Federation member associations. I love giving back to our industry and sharing stories and experiences with other professionals around the globe. I do one or two events a year, schedule permitting as well as doing events for local Toastmasters along the way. Love doing District events when I can too.

# 2012

## 2012: What is your story?

I get people asking how I continually come up with stories for my presentations and my writing. **One thing** is simply to keep an open mind, see and capture observations of activities and things that happen as you go through each day. Guess this has helped as I have done 30 plus publications in various formats from print to EPUB. Wow!

One of the other things you can do is **create a story using a 'TIP' as a foundation or starting point**. This works for speeches as well.

**For example** (taken from **Speaking for Success** 7th Edition)

- The number one principle for success is:
- 2 ways of approaching:
- 3 questions to ask when:
- 4 cornerstones of:
- 5 key elements of:
- 6 steps to creating:
- 7 ways to:
- 8 secrets of:
- 9 lies of myths in the:
- 10 tips when using:

**Using stories** allows you to build bridges with your audience (written or oral) and allow you to share information, ideas, dialogue, concepts, or perhaps even stir up some creative controversy to engage them.

**Using stories** helps start conversations and build relationships which can lead to successful interactions and collaborations.

**Using stories** helps your audience relate to you as a 'real live person' which helps foster good will and better understanding.

Stories help add interest and personality to your writing, presentations, and conversations. Stories are everywhere, just be awake and collect them.

# 2012: Olympics…

As the TV sets of the world tune into London, England (2012) I thought it would be appropriate to touch on the Olympics being hosted there. Lots of excitement, energy, and the work of thousands of volunteers and staff to make it come together and to make it run smoothly.

I'd like to focus on the spirit of the games…

**The Olympic Spirit**
**"…not to win but to take part"**

**The Olympic spirit is best expressed in the Olympic Creed:**
*"The most important thing in the Olympic Games is not to win but to take part, just as the most important thing in life is not the triumph but the struggle. The essential thing is not to have conquered but to have fought well."*

All too often the Olympics *devolves* into politics which cheapens them and the hard work of all the athletes, their coaches, their families, and their supportive communities from their respective countries. **Becoming an Olympian** can be the highlight of an athlete's life, or it can be the *continuation* of their dream to draw from inside to bring out the best of themselves and test themselves in competition with the world's best.

We salute those who created the arenas where these Olympians can test themselves and see what they are fully capable of doing, their coaches, their families, and their supportive communities. Each plays a part in the on-going success of the athletes who take part.

Let me ask you, **"Do you have the heart and spirit of an Olympian?"**

**In the arenas of your daily life, your career, your business, and your relationships – do you strive to fight well, struggle, and maximize your potential success in each arena?**

**Struggle is a part of life**, a valued part. It helps make us stronger, proves our desires and commitments, and keeps us focused on what is truly important in our lives. Struggles are inevitable – and how we deal with them reveals whether we have the heart and spirit of an Olympian or just a dream with no dedication to make it a reality.

# 2012: Commitment

**What are you committed to doing, changing, fine tuning, eliminating, or adding to your life this year?**

The tides come in and washes away all that was built on sand, but what was built on a solid foundation (rock) endures.

Time and tide can also wash away the disappointments and tears over the losses and the mistakes over the past 12 months. **Learn from the lessons** and use them to powerful purpose in this new year. You have before you twelve brand-new, never been used, months to create the life, the business, the career, the relationships you've only dreamt of. Resolve to do them; make a commitment to yourself and live with wild adventure to amaze those who watch you grow.

*"A poor man celebrates the New Year once a year. A rich man celebrates each day. But the richest man celebrates every moment."* **Sri Ravi Shankar**

Whether you made resolutions or not, whether you even stayed up late enough to watch the new year begin, you can start enjoying your riches today.

The riches in your life are so much more than just things and money – I consider myself rich in friends and extended family. I have been blessed with so many outstanding people in my life, like you, that I consider each day a wonder.

# 2012: Point to Ponder – Imagine!

*"Imagine... Here you are, on the high peak of a mountain. You can choose to wing your way toward the clouds, or you can simply walk the usual, ordinary paths that lead to the valley below. Which choice will you make – the well-worn paths or rising above it all? Beautiful things await you if you can reach the heights."* **George Sand**

**Each day we have a choice: we can choose to fly or walk.** Either is fine, but it is good to remember we have made a choice either way. At times, we choose to walk the familiar path and perhaps that is fine when we need to rest or let the routine things of life take a lead. But that is not the choice of those who would make their lives provide a difference.

Do you remember a time when you saw something so exciting that it inspired you to spread your wings and fly? **How did that feel?**

- Was it scary?

- Was it exciting?
- Was it amazing and a time when you truly felt alive?

Our biggest learning experiences often start with setting our vision higher than we are comfortable with and then, despite that discomfort, deciding to push off in pursuit of making them a reality.

During this summer season, why not carve out some time to dream and envision where you could fly if you believed you could and were willing to learn what you needed to make your flight a successful one. Then, as you move into the fall, spread your wings and let yourself fly to greater success, overcoming greater challenges and to leveraged service.

***"Your mind will answer most questions if you learn to relax and wait for the answer."*** **William S. Burroughs**

I'm not sure about you, but this can be my biggest challenge – to *consciously* decide to relax. Sure, I can do it for awhile when I am on holidays sitting by a beach or on a boat, but otherwise my mind whirls with ideas and lists.

My friend, **Robert Stack** shared this question recently on Facebook, **"When was the last time you relaxed?"** I had to admit, it has been a while! Perhaps when we were touring Australia and Hong Kong.

I've been a tad busy since we came home with trips to Montreal and Ottawa. Working on other programs and, even, here at our place in the country, I've been keeping busy. Yes, it has been productive, but lately I have felt a bit ***burned*** out.

While Irene and I are away to BC this month, I am going to *consciously* take time to relax, to read a book, to nap, to spend time chatting with Irene. Just because!

Irene *was* the Chief official (Throws) at the Canadian Nationals (Track and Field) in Calgary at the end of June. I drove down to pick her up on the 30th and we headed to BC on Saturday evening. We stopped in to spend the afternoon and evening with two of our favorite people, Wayne and Brenda, and then continued to Langley on Monday to visit with her aunt.

Wayne is a long-time friend and is a *brilliant* **3C colleague. Cheerleader, Coach and Champion.** I used to detour out of my way to spend some time with him and Brenda when I was still commuting between Edmonton and Vancouver to teach. It has always been worth the journey. Now that Irene and Brenda have connected, it is even more fun. Irene and I love spending time, however brief, with these two friends.

We had such a great time catching up on the deck. Weather was wonderful. After a delicious b-b-q Wayne drove us into Kelowna to see the fireworks. Thanks again Cottons... smile.

Irene's aunt Eva is such a positive lady and a joy in our lives, despite battling cancer. We are moving up our visit to her, just in case.

We hope to spend a few days camping, vegging, and relaxing on the way home. Either way, it will be good to relax and spend some much-needed time doing nothing... smile. I'm packing a few books to help me enjoy my time off. **"When was the last time you relaxed?"**

## 2012: "The Seven Blunders of the World"

This is a list that Gandhi gave to his grandson Arun Gandhi, written on a piece of paper, on their final day together, shortly before his assassination. **The seven blunders he shared are:**

- Wealth without work.
- Pleasure without conscience.
- Knowledge without character.
- Commerce without morality.
- Science without humanity.
- Worship without sacrifice.
- Politics without principle.

**People wonder where I get ideas for my points to ponder.** Well, I got this from a friend on Facebook and thought I would save it to share with you this month. So often we are super busy in our lives, careers, and businesses. Too often we forget what is important to be a true success. We misplace or forget our core commitments and end up losing much more than just our reputation. We lose ourselves and our dreams. That can be the saddest loss of all.

As we move into summer, perhaps, we have a bit more time to relax, refresh, or recharge. During this warmer time of the year, I would challenge you to refine and redirect your energies and expertise to avoid these seven blunders on the road to your success. Invest some of your down time to thinking and dreaming again and then set some new goals for the fall and beyond.

We work hard; our *busy-ness* takes its toll. When we focus our energies in creating experiences and enterprises that provide solid value we move further ahead.

Gandhi also said: **"An ounce of practice is worth more than tons of preaching."**

## 2012: Rise Up!

What are you going to do when you are bullied? **RISE UP!**
What are you going to do when you see someone being bullied? **RISE Up!**
What are you going to do when someone needs protection? **RISE UP!**

**Can you begin to imagine the sound made by 3200 charged up grade 3 to grade 7 students when they stand up and shout at the top of their lungs – 'RISE UP!'?** I can and it was unbelievable and humbling at the same time.

I waited in the team box at floor level at Rexall Place (where the Oilers or the Edmonton Rush sit during their home games) to be introduced, to walk on the field, and to turn and face these 3200 students.

**It was a game changer for me!**

Friday, Feb. 24th the Edmonton Rush lacrosse team hosted these kids for a first ever **Rise UP against Bullying Rally**. I had been asked to share a few words.

I told the students I had been a bit afraid of speaking to them. Why? Because this was not just a speech, this was to kids, and it was important. I told them I remembered being picked on when I was very young and how it made me feel.

I asked if they would allow me to share a few ideas with that 8-year-old version of myself (Robert as I was called then). Would that be ok? **They said yes!**

**Here is some of what I told my 8-year-old self:**

- Get over the expectation that life is fair – it isn't! Things happen and they aren't always good. But you'll get through it because you believe in yourself.
- Don't compare yourself with anyone else. Compare yourself with you from yesterday. How have you grown?
- Celebrate every win, regardless of how small. Do your own happy dance.
- Be somebody and make a difference.
- Take personal leadership and responsibility for your life. Be a leader!
- I ended with the questions used at the start of this article. They responded with an enthusiasm that gave me goosebumps and made my heartbeat even faster.

I found myself speaking with a level of passion not felt for awhile. I found myself rising up and challenging them! They stood up and declared that they would **Rise UP!** And, I believed them! I found myself inspired by their enthusiasm.

**https://youtu.be/tvrHPYLv39Y** Video captured from field level.

As I watch this video, I am struck with the thought that these ideas shared with the 8-year-old me ring as true and valid today and are as needed by the soon to be 63-year old me. Perhaps they ring true for you as well? We need to Rise Up in support of who we are and who we still want to be, of what we want to accomplish in our lives.

**2012:** *"Twenty years from now you will be more disappointed by the things you didn't do than by the ones you did do. So, throw off the bowlines, sail away from the safe harbor. Catch the trade winds in your sails. Explore. Dream. Discover."* **Mark Twain**

When I joined Toastmasters April 1991, I was picking up the pieces from a devastating divorce that had left me battered, bruised, and, perhaps, broken. I was rebuilding and this 'little' dream of becoming a professional speaker re-emerged. It had long been suppressed and dormant. As I began to dream, it came back and called to me... **follow your path, explore, dream, discover**. Like this quote from Mark Twain, I moved out of my comfort zone into what became, for me, the winner's zone.

I joined **Toastmasters of Today** in mid-April of 1991 and found a group of supportive people who encouraged me, educated me, engaged me, and helped me push past my fear into making my dream of **'Speaking my way around the world'** a reality. Thanks, seems so inadequate for where that journey has led.

**Irene and I just returned from 5 weeks of travel** that took us to Hong Kong twice (my 35th country) and a return visit to Australia (my 3rd, her 2nd) where we felt the sand between our toes. Ahhhhhhhhh!

We cried as her daughter Amanda and Michael exchanged vows (April 4th) on Blue Holes beach outside of Kalbarri, Western Australia. What an amazing backdrop for a wedding.

I also had the opportunity of presenting my **Speaking for Success** workshop in Perth for D17 on April 14th. Seventy-one people invested a Saturday afternoon to learn how to be more persuasive and powerful speakers. What an amazing and responsive audience. I love what I do!

Several of those who attended gave us an evening tour of **Freo** (Freemantle to the tourists) where we were staying following the event. We had drinks in one spot, dinner in another, coffee again on 'Cappuccino Row' and wine at another spot on the bay to finish the evening. Thanks guys!

We did some sailing, took a few cruises, lots of beach time, played tourist, saw the dolphins again in Monkey Mia, and even flew to a small island (part of the Abrolhos chain) 60-km off the coast of Geraldton to spend the day exploring, snorkeling, and relaxing. That was a highlight for sure. I even got to fire the ceremonial one o'clock cannon at the Round House in Freo. Overall, we had a great time.

We also flew to Melbourne, Victoria to spend a couple of days with my friend **Lindsay Adams** and his wonderful wife **Debby** to celebrate my birthday.

I first met them when Lindsay was the 2009-2010 International President of the Global Speakers Federation and we got to know each other better when we both spoke at PSA Holland. We had fun and built on that friendship. It was wonderful to be away and to spend time with friends and family in Australia. I must admit we were glad to come home too.

**Hong Kong was amazing and is now on our 'let's go back' list**.

This past year has had its challenges as well as its very pleasant moments and successes. It has been an adventure we've been pleased to share with you.


**2012: Aunt Eva is now doing her gardening in Heaven**. No doubt making it look even better. She completed her journey in the early morning of Sept. 17th. Rest in Peace Aunt Eva.

I was fortunate to be able to visit with her when I flew into BC to speak for the BC CEO Network on the 13th. She was heavily sedated and opened her eyes briefly on my second visit on the way back to the airport. I had the chance to tell her again how much she meant to me and Irene and to remind her that we loved her and would cherish her memory.

She was an amazing woman who thought of others a lot. Imagine our surprise when we got a card from her that **she had her daughter Brenda create prior to her passing**. A card that included a favorite poem of hers and a brief handwritten note. Her instructions to Brenda were to mail the cards after she was gone. I cried and warned Irene that she would cry when she came home. She did. We miss this beautiful soul who loved us and encouraged us whenever we were lucky enough to either chat with her in person or on the phone.

I thought it only fitting to dedicate this month's ezine to this powerful influence in my life. **Her influence lives on in our lives** and I hope in yours. It is called the ripple effect and Aunt Eva proved it every day as she loved people, simply loved them. Here is **the poem that Eva loved and wanted to share** with us...

**To the Ones I Love and Those Who Love Me**

*When I am gone, release me, let me go...*
*I have so many things to see and do*
*Please don't tie yourself to me with tears*
*Be happy that we had these precious years.*
*I gave you my love, you can only guess*
*How much you gave me in happiness*
*I thank you for the love you each have shown*
*But now it's time I travelled on alone.*
*So grieve for me if grieve you must*
*Then let your grief be comforted by trust.*
*It's only for awhile that we must part*
*So bless the memories within your heart.*
*I won't be far away, and life goes on*
*So if you need me, call me and I will come.*
*Though you won't see me or touch me, I'll be there*
*And if you listen with your heart, you'll hear*
*All my love around you soft and clear.*
*And then, when you must come this way alone,*
*I'll greet you with a smile and say*
*"Welcome Home".*

Papyrus, the makers of the blank card that Brenda used to create Eva's final words, included a card which said, **"Legends say the hummingbirds float free of time, carrying our hopes for love, joy and celebration.**

**The hummingbird's delicate grace reminds us that life is rich, beauty is everywhere, every personal connection has meaning, and laughter is life's sweetest creation."** They must have known Eva.

So, next year when the hummingbirds return to our garden, I will be reminded again of this beautiful woman who was a gift in my life. We will remember you Aunt Eva.

## 2012: Smart man, Albert Einstein!

Read an article where Albert shared 10 tips. Each of these tips can be relevant for us in various stages and situations in life. Each has a nucleus of wisdom we can use to power ourselves through whatever challenge we face.

**I like #5: Make mistakes.** Because I often do; bet you do too. However, I have learned to reflect on those mistakes and see what lesson I can extract and leverage to help me as I move along my journey. Often, my mistakes have given me something of real value to share with my readers, audiences, and colleagues.

**I also like #7: Create Value.** Value is what separates us from our competition. Perceived value is what allows us to profitably build and enhance our careers, companies, and communities.

**How about #4: The imagination is powerful**. Most of the amazing things in our world started in someone's imagination. Perhaps you imagined something, invested time to research and study it, and then went out and made it a reality. Wonderful to see it become real!

I figure you're all smart enough to draw your own conclusions on these tips but wanted to share a few ideas with you.

 **"If a cluttered desk is a sign of a cluttered mind, then what are we to think of an empty desk?"** 😊

## 2012: *"Creativity is intelligence having fun."* Albert Einstein

Think I have already mentioned my trip to Tehran in an earlier note. I loved the opportunity to meet the people of Iran and to get a taste of their culture. I found a responsive audience of people who were so open to learn and share their experience with me. I am blessed.

I was amazed that people would line up for quite a while to get my autograph and talk with me. And many of them wanted a hug and a picture. Felt like a real rock star… 😊 I fully enjoyed my 8 days in Iran and wish them well as they find their place in the world.

## 2012: Amanda and Michael married on the beach

Irene's daughter, **Amanda** is a teacher. Teaching positions are scarce here in Alberta, so she took one in Geraldton, Western Australia. She met **Michael Burgess** on-line as they were both on-line gamers.

In fact, he found the posting for the school that hired her before she even moved there.

We went to visit her and spent some time with them. I remember telling Irene, "She is not coming home soon."

When, she announced they were getting married, **April 4th** on the beach. We said, we knew. We were pleased to be able to be there for her and to support them as they started their new life together. Michael is an amazing young man who we both love and respect immensely. We will be back for more visits.

## 2012: People ask where I get the creative sparks for my writing.

Simple, I just keep my eyes open and ask questions.

**For example,** earlier this past week I mentioned to Irene that there was a wasp inside the hummingbird feeder outside our kitchen window. The hummers were gone but somehow this wasp (yellow jacket/hornet) had been able to crawl in. She said she had seen it the day before and it was dead. I told her; no, it wasn't. I had just noticed it swimming on top of the sugar water.

Later that day I looked out and it was still swimming. I noticed the water level had dropped. My observation, the wasp continuing to swim was pushing the water out through the 4 'flower' openings. His fellow wasps were coming to take advantage of it. I checked back a couple more times that day and the levels were still dropping, and the wasp was still swimming.

For the record, after being stung last year (Irene – twice and me – once) and being inundated with thousands of these nasty insects – I HATE WASPS!

I love to trap and kill them, as I did literally thousands last year. Despite that, I had to admire this wasp's determination to live and find a way out. The next morning the wasp was gone and so was all the sugar water. Hmmmm!

**Determination is a success trait and one we can acquire.** For example, this is my 114th issue since we started so many years ago. There have been times I wanted to quit, but then I would get a note from one of our readers and it would inspire me to continue.


## 2012: Sometimes our words grow wings

I can't remember when I first shared these words, but this quote has gone viral on the internet over the years. Shown here, with my friend **Richard Mulvey** in the **"Bob Hooey" training room** in Johannesburg, South Africa.

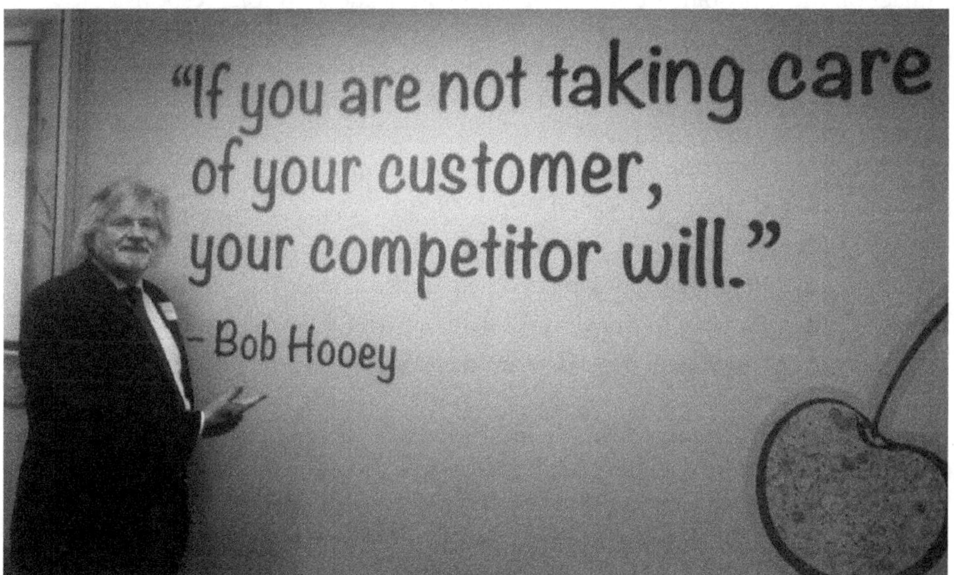


I've included it in several of my books. It has been quoted in **Fast Company** and **Inc! Magazine** among others. I've even seen other companies quoting it, creating memes and posting on-line.

It makes me smile when it is quoted, used as a meme, or printed, and I appreciate that people are being reminded of what is important in business around the globe.

# 2013

**2013: Thought I would share a tidbit from the 2nd edition of 'Legacy of Leadership,' Strive for significance – lead on purpose!**

My view is that we each have **personal leadership and responsibility** for our lives, our actions, and our decisions. That personal leadership may extend to volunteer or paid leadership. Our success or ***significance*** as a leader is based on taking 100% responsibility for what happens in our lives and as a result of our choices.

**A leadership review or check-up**

Reflect on these probing questions around your leadership role, responsibility, and skills. Briefly record your thoughts. Being honest in recognizing your strengths and focused areas of growth is one of the characteristics of the top-level leaders. Asking for help or getting coaching is another success characteristic.

- What is your personal vision for your leadership role?
- What are your specific areas of responsibility?
- What strengths and skills do you bring to the role?
- What leadership areas do you need help in developing?
- Where do you need to draw on the skills of your fellow leaders or employees?
- Perhaps engage a leadership or team development coach.

**I also shared this piece about Teamwork.** As leaders, what we are looking for is team effectiveness. We want our teams to work together and hopefully they will get along, too. But the bottom line is we need for them to be effective in their individual efforts (as a part of the team) and move ahead in the desired direction. That is where we, as leaders, play such an important role.

**Teamwork doesn't work!**

**Teamwork often FAILS** because most organizations use committees, not teams, and don't realize the difference. **Lead on purpose – strive for significance** vs. simply seeking success. What can you do, as the leader, to help your teams grow together and hone their individual skills? Each team member has different drives, dreams, and challenges. Your role is to help them win!

# 2013: Point to Ponder – Whew!

**I celebrated with a Pepsi** (I know I needed to watch my sugars and my calories, but it was so worth it) as I sat on our front deck and realized it was 'finally' finished.

Once again, I played **Bob-the-builder;** and once again it was a major lesson in patience and progress. I had planned to simply redo the deck surface in preparation for redesigning the rails; a similar project to what we did for our front deck. However, when I tore off the siding on the north and south sides so I could see how it was supported... boy was I in for a surprise. A big, scary surprise.

Our mudroom addition (built by one of the previous owners) was not at all well supported. **Under-statement!** So, the project instantly became a larger one.

Tore out the old steps and supports that were rotten and dug out the dirt and junk. Put in a load of sand and gravel in preparation for using two railway ties for support of two new pony walls to support the mudroom. Then, with the help of a neighbor, we jacked up the mudroom addition two inches at the front and installed the two new pony walls I'd built... whew!

I decided to use the space beneath the mudroom for storage and proceeded to build a nice dry storage shed to house my rototiller and mower in the winter, as well as what ever else that will fit. This clears out the back storage shed for storage. And, now the door doesn't stick in the winter.

It took 3 weeks of digging, crawling, crouching (in a 36-inch-high space) and it was finished today! **So, I had a Pepsi to celebrate and let my body relax.**

**Small victories are important too!** They bring us the same satisfactions as larger ones and maybe even a lesson or two along the way.

Now, I know I could have hired someone to do this for us, and it would have been much easier on my 'old' body; but I had the time this summer and I am learning to be a handy guy around the house. Building something with my hands brings a whole new source of satisfaction and learning. **What have you done lately to stretch and to build?** What have you done lately to build your business or enhance your career?

## 2013: Today, I have been 'alive' 23608 days – 3372 weeks and 3 days

I would love to say I have 'lived' each day, But, like many, I did not fully appreciate or embrace each day as I encountered it.

- How long have you been on this earth? Work it out!
- How many of the days you have been alive have you 'lived'?
- How many of them have been days in which you fully embraced to make memorable in your life and in the lives of others?
- What will you change to ensure that each day going forward becomes one in which you live and make a difference?

With a new year approaching this might be a good time to consider what you want to do with the rest of your life. With this being a time for many of us to spend with family or miss those we've lost, again a time of reflection.

May this Christmas season be one where you enjoy the real gifts of friendship, fellowship, and fun. And may next year be one that blows your mind with adventure and achievement.


## 2013: Do you have a good connection?

If you have a bad connection, you have problems. Understatement for sure!

I was coming home early last month and stopped at the mailbox to check the mail. Got back in the old Dodge and went to start it and saw the lights go dark. Everything went black. No power, no current, not even click or a grrrrrr of a straining starter. I walked home (thankfully only a couple of blocks, brrrrrrr) and called my friend and neighbor **Kelly Bigoray**, who is a mechanic.

After both of us had our dinners, I took the Saturn down and we were able to finally charge it enough to start the car and drive it to the garage. Kelly did some diagnostics and figured the battery was ok and the alternator was fine... but, it still wasn't charging... Kelly continued looking. Kelly took off the leads to the battery and cleaned the posts and replaced the positive lead. It has run well since then... simple fix to a perplexing problem.

All that was stopping the battery from getting a charge was a bad connection. Once that was fixed everything worked as it should. Funny thing the connection looked ok from the outside but was obviously not working.

In life and more so in business our *connections* are the lifeblood of our continued growth and success. We cannot afford to take them for granted. They need to be checked, tested, and perhaps cleaned or polished from time to time. Until next time, keep your connections flowing.


**2013: Eleanor Roosevelt** wrote, *"I have never given very deep thought to a philosophy of life, though I have a few ideas that I think are useful to me. One is that you do whatever comes your way to do as well as you can, and another is that you think as little as possible about yourself and as much as possible about other people and about things that are interesting. The third is that you get more joy out of giving joy to others and should put a good deal of thought into the happiness that you are able to give."*

**Interesting concept, isn't it?**

- **Do your best**
- **Focus on others and interesting thing**
- **Give happiness to others**

Sounds like a recipe for a full and fulfilling life. Sounds like a recipe for a productive and profitable career or business too.

Too often we get bogged down, burnt out, and/or physically and mentally challenged with the day-to-day challenges of life. That is normal and something we need to be aware. It's ok to take a break to recharge, refocus, and reframe our lives and our commitments. Give yourself permission to relax once in awhile.

At times, I find I do need to step out of my own head and think about interesting things, or to refocus my energies on helping others (this feeds me). Although sometimes I just have to do my best with what I have. Wishing you a productive and happy year.


## 2013: Getting started

*"The secret of getting ahead is getting started. The secret to getting started is breaking your complex overwhelming tasks into small manageable tasks and then starting on the first one."* **Mark Twain**

Somehow, I have always liked the concept of the waves coming in and cleaning the beach.

Out with the old and in with the new, clean, uncluttered sand. Something wonderful about the sound of the surf and the touch of the sun on my face.

**Each year we get the chance to start over** (actually, each day) with a clean slate and an open, creative mind. We can visualize what we want to accomplish, then start building solid foundations beneath it. When you build on a solid foundation, what you build has a better chance to survive the tests and trials that will un-doubtedly come against it. When you build on shaky sand, well... you know the rest.

**What do you want to build this year?**

- A stronger, more healthy body?
- A stronger, more loving relationship?
- A stronger, more profitable business?
- A stronger, more productive career?
- A stronger, more expansive network?

These are only a few of the questions you might want to ask as you move into this new year. **But they are only a part of the equation you need to succeed.**

- What do you need to do, change, or acquire to make them real?
- Who do you need to ask for help to make them come alive?
- What do you need to let go of, to confidently move forward?
- What habits do you need to either acquire or defeat to win?
- Where do you need to start?
- When will you start?
- What checklists or accountability points do you need in place?

## 2013: Point to Ponder

**Have you ever wondered about something you observed?**

I was sitting on our front deck last week having lunch when I noticed some blurred action in one of our evergreens. I saw something on one branch, drop down to a second one, turn upside down, and fall to a third one.

A minute or so later I saw this very young robin fly up and settle on one of the branches in our lilac hedge. There he sat! Despite his parents calls, encouragement, and even coming close to him, there he sat, and sat, and sat.

I remarked to Irene about this young bird and wondered out loud if he continued to sit because he was scared from his fall, embarrassed (guy thing) or was just waiting to get his energy and his courage up to try again.

We have two nesting pairs of robins and one of the nests is in the upper part of the tree next to this one. The branches overlap and perhaps he simply fell out of the nest.

Not sure what happened as I finished lunch and went back in to get some more work done. He wasn't there the next time I came out so perhaps he made up his mind and flew back home. Or, perhaps he jumped down to the deck and just walked back.

Made me think about you and me when we encounter something like this. It doesn't work like we planned, or it takes us by surprise. What we do then, defines how we live and how well we live.

- Do we let our fears control us?
- Do we let our fear of being embarrassed stop us?
- Do we catch our breath, refocus on the sky, and fly again?

In each case the choice is ours. There are people in your life who are there to encourage you and to coach you, if you will let them.


## 2013: Are you happy?

*"The happiest people are those who think the most interesting thoughts. Interesting thoughts can only live in cultivated minds. Those who decide to use leisure as a means of mental development, who love good music, good books, good pictures, good plays at the theater, good company, good conversation – what are they? They are the happiest people in the world; and they are not only happy themselves, but they are also the cause of happiness in others."* **William Lyon Phelps**

This month I encountered and engaged a wide range of people across Canada. Some were happy, some were sad, some were worried, and some were glad when their problems were solved.

**For example:** On our way home from speaking and exploring in Nova Scotia we encountered severe weather when we were attempting to land in Hamilton. We were just about there and had to divert to Ottawa to wait until the airline could assess a plan of action.

It was very interesting listening to the reactions of our fellow travelers. Irene and I travel a bit so we simply took it as it came and hoped we would eventually get back into Hamilton and perhaps find our connecting flight to Edmonton there or hopefully coming in. This is just what happened.... end-result, we were 3 hours late getting into Edmonton and a bit more tired the next day.

On Saturday we met **Yvonne** (*the human vitamin*) at our Speaking for Success Boot Camp. Yvonne is a fitness trainer who wants to be a better speaker. She blew us away with her very first speech. She was *happiness in motion* and brought her vibrant energy to the room. At the end of her presentation, we all felt better. **Are you happy? The choice is yours!**


## 2013: Lessons from the bathroom

I recently returned from a trip to Ottawa, Ontario where I was the closing keynote for a national food and beverage conference. Thanks to CSCM for bringing me in to share a few ideas on productivity and having more 'fun' time at work.

Visited the **Vimy memorial sculptures** on display at the War Museum in Ottawa where we went for cocktails.

Great to see our tax dollars at work where they support something of value.

The conference was held at the Delta City Centre hotel. Nice facility and great staff. Great audience as well.

*Pictured here - the real thing the model is crafted to portray, that Irene and I visited in person!*

I found some delightful soaps and shampoo bottles in my bathroom. I brought them home as a keepsake. **Let me explain why.** Each of them had something of value to spark my thinking and get me going for the day. I loved their shared philosophy and that a hotel would invest in them 'just' for me.
**I share 4 of them with you with my thoughts:**

**Celebrate life (shampoo)**
**Philosophy: Every day is a gift waiting to be opened**

Interestingly, I was speaking with them (CSCM) about liberating time to allow them to lead and to enjoy their lives more fully. When we treat each day as a gift and an adventure to be lived, we get more from it as we move through it.

**Celebrate dreams (shower gel)**
**Philosophy: when you need to feel like your heart has wings, dream big**

I remember meeting with **Peter J. Daniels** in Adelaide, Australia when I first started down this professional speaking path. He challenged me to dream bigger so that I would have the necessary motivation to work through the challenges and detours I would encounter. He was so right! What drives you is what will help you on your path to a more successful, fulfilling life.

**Be somebody (body lotion)**
**Philosophy: the headlines you make in life will be based on the difference you make in the lives of others**

Each of us is somebody who can make a difference where we choose. When you invest in the lives of others, you expand both your service and your influence. This is where you make the biggest difference. Give it forward!

**Celebrate love (conditioner)**
**Philosophy: celebrate those who fill your cup and love you unconditionally**

Too often we forget to thank and to celebrate those who are important in our lives. When we do that, we rob them and ourselves of the joy of knowing the difference they make in our lives, A small gesture or token of affection can make a major difference. I try to remind Irene how special she is and how much she means to me on a regular basis. Remember and celebrate them today.

**How amazing is this;** to invest in your guests by encouraging them to celebrate life, to dream, to be someone, and to love.


## 2013: I am asked how I was able to create the amazing wins in my life.

I simply state, **"If I can do it, so can you!"** If you have the dreams and the inner desire and are willing to be disciplined and focus your energies and mindset, you can easily surpass what I have done, so far. **"Big dreams coupled with strategic steps lead to significant success!"**

One such dream was becoming a professional speaker who traveled the world **offering help and hope to people who needed an inspirational nudge.**

**I joined Toastmasters in 1991** to begin equipping myself to walk this adventurous path. Along the way I earned recognition for my leadership and speaking. I was the 48th speaker world-wide to earn their professional level **Accredited Speaker** designation and was inducted into their Hall of Fame. Later, I began successfully sharing my ideas and speeches with associations and companies. This was followed by publishing articles and, later, books that have found eager readers and leaders around the globe.

Along the way, **I discovered an affinity for leaders.** I've been privileged to offer them encouragement and work with them to productively equip and motivate their teams to profitably grow and win. Love the folks I serve!

**I'm also asked how I keep positive and focused.** On *home* days, I am awakened by our furry kids. I get up, feed them, do a few stretches, read something positive and reflect on the game plan set the night before. I choose to write prior to digging into other projects such as presentation prep for a client or one of my charity events. My 30 plus books were an act of desire and discipline. On *road* days my routine is similar without the furry alarm clocks.

There are also days where I need a nudge or boost. This is where I touch base with a select group of friends like my cheerleader **Kim Yost** (who continues to challenge me), some of my Toastmasters or CAPS/NSA colleagues, and my wife Irene (*who often quotes me to me*) to be encouraged. Then I dig back into my work.

*Bob and Kim Yost preparing to honor our friend **Bill Comrie** in Ontario where he was awarded Retailer of the year.*

**My greatest joy is seeing my Ideas At Work within an organization and seeing people take personal leadership, play to their strengths, and thrive.**

I work diligently to create something significant to enhance my brand and ability to help people grow and win. I love what I do and plan on staying healthy to do it well into my mid or late 80's. God willing, of course.

**Success is a choice you make each day.** Each day you can choose to create BIG dreams and focus on the strategic steps that will make them a vivid reality. Each decision acted upon helps to create a lifetime of success and significance. **Say YES, you can!**

A shorter version of this point to ponder will be featured in my friend **Kim Yost's** new book **'iPump'** being released in June. It will lead off his chapter two.

## 2013: Determination is a success trait and one we can acquire.

For example, this is my 114th issue since we started so many years ago. There have been times I wanted to quit, but then I would get a note from one of our readers and it would inspire me to continue.

**In yesterday's news** (Mon. Sept 2nd) I read that 64-year-old U.S. endurance swimmer **Diana Nyad** waded ashore Monday in Key West, Fla and became the first person to swim from Cuba to Florida without the help of a shark cage. A 53-hour swim that I couldn't imagine even attempting. She is my age, and she is a very courageous woman. I'm sure lots of people told her she was crazy to attempt this swim. However, I'm sure she had some, including those who helped her, who believed in her and encouraged her to swim. This was her 5th and final attempt.

**As Diana said on the beach,** *"I have three messages. One is, we should never, ever give up. Two is, you're never too old to chase your dream. Three is, it looks like a solitary sport, but it is a team."*

I echo Diana's hard-won words of wisdom. What can you do with your life, regardless of what age and what circumstances you face?

**When will you jump in and start swimming?**

*"Failure will never overtake me if my determination to succeed is strong enough."* **Og** Mandino

I have read every book Og wrote and subscribed to Success Unlimited which he edited for years. Even got to hear him speak along with my friend **Peter J. Daniels** one year in Vancouver. He is gone now, but his influence in my life continues.

**It doesn't seem like 5 years have come and gone, but they have.** I've shared this story before, but I love telling it. On Sept. 30th somewhere off the coast of either Oregon or California I asked Irene to marry me. She said yes and that made my life so much better. We were on a repositioning cruise from Vancouver to LA, her first cruise. (***Update 2019:*** *The first of many we were to share around the world.*)

Our next stop from LA was Las Vegas. I wasn't sure if we could get married there, as both of us had been married previously.

I phoned a speaker colleague and his wife and asked her to check it out. Turns out it was easy to do, so we did! We both bought new outfits to get married in and I was able to find a nice little wedding ring. Our friends drove us down and acted as our official witnesses.

We were married by an ordained preacher in a small wedding chapel off the strip. Irene's only request was no drive through and no Elvis. There was an Elvis in the building doing a wedding for another couple. ☺ We flew home to Edmonton as man and wife later that evening.

**It has been an interesting 5 years together, so far.** I can only speak for myself, but my life was made immensely better when Irene became a permanent part of it. She has become so much more than just my wife. She is my partner, my proof-reader, researcher, encourager, champion, coach at times, and my cheerleader and at times, my butt kicker. I trust I have been able to add to her life as well.

Together we have created new websites, business ventures, published a number of books including **Legacy of Leadership**. We've traveled the world, cruising, touring, snorkeling and exploring (and we are not even close to being done yet). We've watched her daughter marry a very nice young Aussie. We have laughed, cried, loved, even argued at times; but through it all we have grown closer together. I can honestly say I love her more now than when we were wed 5 years ago. I am looking forward to whatever life holds for us. I hope I am here and in-my-mind able to re-negotiate our 30-year agreement. (*Fun idea we had... smile*)


## 2013: 13 steps, a shaky start

The night was dark, it was raining, and the wind was howling. There were 13 steps, in a darkened outside entrance from the dimly lit parking lot, down into the basement meeting room. How did I know? I counted them as I went down, went back up, and, then, *screwed up* my courage and went back down again.

I descended slowly, hesitantly for the second time, reached out and nervously placed my hand on the doorknob. My heart was pumping (fast ☺), my legs were shaky, and my breathing was short and labored. Was I making the right decision?

What would I find on the other side of the door? Maybe I should just turn around and go home? How would I react? Whose crazy idea was this anyway? Would they like me, help me, or reject me? ***"Ok, Hooey, go for it!"***

I *forced* a smile on my face, turned the knob, and opened the door. I stood for a minute, took a deep breath, and stepped into Vancouver based ***Toastmasters of***

**_Today!_ I made that first step that has taken me around the world sharing my message of help and hope!**

I still remember my first visit that Tuesday night in April 1991. I was _nervous_ and shy. Now, anyone who knows me will find that hard to believe, but it was very true, back then. This was a scary moment for me as I had just come through a devastating and debilitating divorce. Frankly, I didn't feel very _confident in myself_ or my abilities. If you're a Toastmaster, remember your first visit to your club. Perhaps, like me, you felt a little nervous or intimidated by members who could get up and seemingly speak without notes or nervousness.

I was there, reviving a dream of being a professional speaker and someday being able to stand on the big stage sharing my ideas, travelling the world, and inspiring and investing in the lives of those in the audience.

What I found at the bottom of those 13 steps was a supportive, friendly group of people who befriended me and became my champions, coaches, and cheerleaders; some of whom still play that role today.

- Perhaps you have had a similar experience as you began something?
- Perhaps you are feeling a bit shaky about starting down this path to becoming a better speaker? Perhaps you too want to be a professional speaker?
- Perhaps you have played a similar role in the growth of a Toastmaster member or business friend?

That **one step** into the room, following the 13 down made an amazing difference in my life and my career. (**_Update 2019:_** _I have now been a professional speaker for 25 plus years and have visited 61 countries on 6 continents, speaking in 24, so far._)

In 1998, I had the _distinct_ pleasure of walking across a Palm Desert, California stage to be inducted into the Toastmasters International Hall of Fame as the 48th professional level Accredited Speaker in our rich history. (**_Update 2019:_** _There are now 87 AS who have earned this coveted professional level designation._)

In 2008, I had the _rare_ privilege of keynoting the leadership luncheon at the Toastmasters International convention. As part of my introduction, they played the video of me walking across that Palm Desert stage. My first words were, **"_I may have walked across that stage by myself… but I did not get there by myself?_"**

- It took those first 13 steps, **_plus_** the loving, supportive investment of thousands of fellow Toastmasters, CAPS, GSF, and NSA colleagues, over many years, to help move me toward that goal.

- It took those first 13 steps to start me on the path to living my dream of travelling the world sharing ideas and challenging people to reach out and build foundations of success under their dreams.

**Update 2013:** In 2011, I was selected as one of 300 Toastmasters International Ambassadors around the globe appointed as influencers to help with the launch of the first re-brand in their history. I was glad to serve and give back to this amazing organization. In 2013, I was appointed one of Toastmasters Learning Masters as we worked to revitalize our educational programs.

## 2013: Global Speakers Summit – international foundation evening

**This was my last event, year 5 in a 3-year term.**

I agreed to stay on the CAPS Foundation board for one more year to create and host this 2013 Global Speakers Federation event in Vancouver, BC.

It was an amazing experience and one I will cherish!

It was quite a lot of work crafting the theme, **"The Music, The Magic & The Movement."** It was daunting recruiting our musicians and magicians and setting the live and silent auction with donors throughout the GSF. But it came together, and we had a very productive and fun evening. We raised quite a bit of money for CAPS as well as for each of the GSF associations who had been involved in this event.

One lesson I am constantly re-learning is **the power of focused application in the direction of my dreams.** I admit, I get distracted at times. At times I find myself chasing shiny objects or projects that look exciting or at least more fun than the task in front of me. When I return to my task with renewed focus and energy miracles happen. They can happen for you when you focus on your quest and then work diligently to see it come to fruition. You can do it!

My challenge to them was to either add what we had raised on their behalf to their own foundation or use it as seed money to start their own. In subsequent years we saw several begin – hence 'The Movement' part of our theme.

My friends **The Passing Zone, Jon and Owen,** surprised me with a walk on during my introductory remarks and were nice enough to include me in one of their dangerous acts.  Here is the clip from that part of our evening. **https://youtu.be/EqAfczlVMIg**  to see what we did together.

*I had this hand made top hat (above) for the evening's theme… and decided to use this as the theme for this book.*


## 2013: Starting Points

On one of my trips to speak in Holland, I stayed a week longer to explore Denmark and Sweden.

*This picture is in the centre of a big mall adjacent to the town hall in **Copenhagen** and the post marks the exact centre of the city. All measurements are calculated from this post.*

In life we need something or somewhere to mark our starting point so we can track our progress and evaluate how we are doing. Do you have such a starting point?

I challenge you to do so today and then check back to see how you did!
You'll be amazed at your progress.

*"Successful people maintain a positive focus in life no matter what is going on around them. They stay focused on their past successes rather than their past failures, and on the next action steps they need to take to get them closer to the fulfillment of their goals rather than all the other distractions that life presents to them." Jack Canfield*

# 2014

**2014: Point to Ponder "They made me cry!"**

Irene's first words to me when I stopped in Airdrie to pick her up following her being a combined events referee for the **2014 Alberta Summer Games** were, **"They made me cry!"**

**Here is the story behind those words.**

"For all who despair of the youth of our country, know that there is much to be inspired about in them. One of my volunteer occupations is that of an Athletics official. Athletics, for those who don't know, is also known as the sport of track and field.

At the 2014 Alberta Summer games, I was working as the Combined Events Referee. When athletes compete in combined events, they do multiple events over 1 or 2 days, scoring points by their accomplishments in each event. The best known of these is the decathlon for men and the heptathlon for women. For these games, one group of young men was competing in an octathlon: eight events over 2 days. Although the athletes compete against each other, they cheer on the accomplishments and victories of their fellow competitors.

I followed these young men as they competed, getting to know them as I gave them their point totals for the event, how they were placing, and answering their questions about the events. The second day, during the 6th event, one competitor rolled his ankle in the high jump and needed medical attention. His fellow competitors waited patiently after their warmup for the next event and cheered him on when he came back to the group. I overheard them telling him that if he decided to do the final event, the 1000 metre run, they would help him out, even carry him to make sure he finished. I thought, *"Right, that would happen."*

At the line for the 1000 metre run, all the competitors were there for the starter's gun. I watched the race, clearly seeing the pain in the injured competitor's eyes as he raced by me, but he kept on going. Then, someone went down, 600 meters into the race. Not the injured athlete, but another. At the end of the race, the medical staff was looking after 2 athletes, the one who had previously been injured – who completed his race on sheer determination – and this second athlete.

When the medical staff gave him an okay to try to stand, it was his fellow competitors who helped him up.

Then hanging on to him, they brought him to the finish line and then one lap around the track so he could complete his race. At times they carried him, at times he hopped, but as he approached the finish line again, a roar went up in the stands. What sportsmanship! What a testament to these young men. **I had tears in my eyes as they crossed the finish line, all of them with beaming smiles on their faces.**

They had proven that they would stand by their promise to their fellow competitors. When accepting their medals, the winners called all the other competitors to the podium. As they said, by completing this event, we are all winners. We who watched these young men were the true winners that day."

**Irene Gaudet (www.vitrakcreative.com)**


## 2014: Needing Others

**Many living things need each other to survive.** If you have ever seen a Colorado aspen tree, you may have noticed that it does not grow alone. Aspens are found in clusters or groves.

The reason is that the aspen sends up new shoots from the roots. In a small grove, all the trees may be connected by their roots! Giant California redwood trees may tower 300 feet into the sky. It would appear to most that they require extremely deep roots to anchor them against strong winds.

We're told that their roots are quite shallow – to capture as much surface water as possible. And they spread in all directions, intertwining with other redwoods. Locked together in this way, all the trees support each other in wind and storms. Like the aspen, they never stand-alone. They need one another to survive.

**People, too, are connected by a system of roots.** We are born to family and learn early to make friends. We are not meant to survive long without others. And like the redwood, we need to hold one another up. When pounded by the sometimes-vicious storms of life, we need others to support and sustain us.

Have you been going it alone? Maybe it's time to let someone else help hold you up for a while. Or perhaps someone needs to hang on to you.

*Not sure who penned this, Author Unknown, but thought it worth sharing.*

Perhaps this little poem would give you a sense of what it means to work together and the importance of our connections.

Building a world class business and/or an effective team isn't easy, and it isn't done alone. There are other people around who can help – seek them out and ask.

## 2014: George Sidor February 16, 1928 – April 7th, 2014

**For the second time in my life, I lost a man I called 'Dad'.**

Irene's dad left us early on the morning of April 7th; he was 86.

This was a blow to all of us who knew and loved him. He played an important role in so many lives, including mine.

**George was a gentle, loving man who made me feel special**. I will miss him as I still miss my own dad.

I had the privilege of delivering his eulogy and was able to choke back my tears as I sought to honor this **man who loved so well**.

- He loved his wife of 61 years... right to the moment of his passing.
- He loved his 3 kids and worked to provide for them doing whatever he could.
- He loved to spend time with and spoil his grandchildren.
- He loved and welcomed me into his family – even before Irene made it official.
- He loved and was active in his church and his community.
- He loved to laugh, to travel, to build, and to fish.
- He loved to take pictures (we'll be creating a website later this year to showcase them at www.georgesidorphotographer.info) as he was very good at it.
- He loved to share ideas and to enjoy his life. I cherish the times we just sat and talked.

**My challenge for you:** Have you recently told those you love that you love them? Time flies and we never know when they will be taken from us.
I remind Irene that I love her on a regular basis... guess my Alzheimer's is here early but I want to make sure she knows.

**2014: Irene's mom, Lil Sidor finally moved into her new home at Heritage House in Vegreville.**

An opening came up and we jumped on it. Alex came out with his truck, and we moved a great number of furniture pieces into her new one-bedroom apartment.

I spent the morning arranging and hanging pictures while Irene drove over to Two Hills where Lil had been placed on an emergency basis. It was a bit of a rush, but we wanted to make it as much like home as we could and to be a place where she could make new friends and create some new memories.

The look of amazement on her face as Irene wheeled her in made all the hard work more than worth while. I laughed as she kept asking about various pieces of furniture and was able to tell her that, yes... it all came from her home. I think she likes it there as she had several friends already living there who came to visit when she moved in. She has become a bingo winner, and we are thinking of changing her name to **Lucky Lil**.

Our hope is she will have many happy years in her new home. We are working on cleaning out her home (even had a garage sale on the 4th and another one planned for the 19th) so we can sell it for her. (*sadly, we lost her later that year*)

**2014:** *"Leadership,"* says **Peter Drucker**, *"is lifting a person's vision to higher sights, raising a person's performance to a higher standard, and building a personality beyond its normal limitations."* **Now that is creative vision!**

The foundations of effective, personal leadership whether in a business, a career, or leading a volunteer group, start with 'each' person actively taking responsibility for their own actions as part of a group. Personal leadership precedes powerful, effective leadership in any role.

Those foundations are enhanced in feeling confident enough to suggest and create ideas and accept revisions in team goals and performance.

You might be asking, *"What does leadership have to do with creativity and innovation?"* Frankly, everything! If we are to successfully learn new styles of applied problem-solving, unlock our creativity, and increase our ability to make better decisions, more creative decisions; we must be willing to take personal leadership in using them in our own activities and in the interaction with our fellow workers, team members, and clients.

*"Our productivity – often survival – does not depend solely on how much effort we expend, but on whether or not the effort we invest is in the right direction."* We must create visionary, innovative road maps that will guide us and our colleagues to greater success.

**Peter Drucker** also said, *"Management is doing things right; Leadership is doing the right things."* That means **creating better options to precede our decisions and their implementation**. Our goal in effectively handling major problems, challenges, and mistakes is being able to cut through to the root causes and then creatively develop real innovative solutions to put into action.

My objective in writing and rewriting *'Why Didn't I THINK of That? The creative power of Ideas at Work!'* was to assist my readers in acquiring new problem-solving models and introducing a few creativity nudges and tools that will help them in their personal life, career, and interaction with their clients and co-workers.

Through my various books and newsletters, I hope to help you discover a new creative approach and mindset to the problems you may encounter. I challenge you to see them as creative opportunities to grow and change the way you live and/or do business.

This has been a challenging month with continuing family issues. In spite of that, with the completion and launch of **'Why Didn't I THINK of That?** we have still been able to move forward to create something of value for our audiences and readers; and that helps, a lot.


*"Look up at the stars and not down at your feet. Try to make sense of what you see and wonder about what makes the universe exist."* **Stephen Hawking**

**2014: Irene Gaudet was honored as the 2013 Official of the Year by Athletics Alberta on February 8th at a special awards banquet.**

**Athletics Alberta's 2013 Alberta Official of the Year.**

"As the parent of a competing athlete, **Irene Gaudet** offered to help at a track and field meet. Now, approximately 12 years later, she has achieved level 5 in throws, level 3 as a throws referee and level 3 in horizontal jumps. In her capacity as a throws official she has worked 4 consecutive National Championship events - 2009 and 2010 in Toronto and 2011 and 2012 in Calgary. This is an achievement that only a few officials can match! Irene credits much of her early development as a throws official to the 'awesome' mentoring she received from Estella Rung and Peter Hesketh.

She is now doing the same for many of our up-and-coming throws officials.

Since 2006, Irene has also been a valued member of the Alberta Official's Sub-Committee. She is the committee's statistician and coordinates the information related to provincial upgrading applications." *(As printed in the awards magazine.)*

I was glad to be there to cheer her on and to take some pictures of her being honored provincially by her peers for her amazing commitment over all these years. She has always been my amazing wife... now she is an award winning one as well.

She is an amazing lady dealing with all the challenges and activities in her life, taking care of her aging parents, helping guide her kids, supporting and encouraging her husband in his projects, being active in the union movement, as well as working full time and doing her own part time web design and publications coaching business. And, with all of this, she still has time to work with Athletes from across the Province and the country. **Bravo my love!**

## 2014: Applying the 4 H's of leadership

Monday, November 2nd I had the chance to meet, chat and share lunch with
**Mohammed Mura, DTM,** our current International President for Toastmasters
International.

Mohammed was spending 6 weeks traveling the globe visiting some of our
Toastmasters Districts. This week he was visiting D42 and was our special guest
this weekend at our fall convention in Calgary.

**Toastmasters is celebrating its 90th anniversary this year.**

I found him a very gracious man who was very open to all who attended the
lunch. During lunch he shared a few ideas on his vision of leadership. From my
memory, here is what he shared with us, entitled the 4 H's.

- He talked about using our **HEAD** as leaders and the importance of thinking
  as well as acting.
- He talked about engaging our **HEART** and leading with compassion.
- He talked about the importance of good **HEALTH** and its impact on being
  able to be effective leaders.
- He talked about how the most impactful, effective leaders lead with
  **HUMILITY**.

A short session but one that resonated with me as I seek to serve and equip committed leaders and their teams to grow and succeed.

I gave him copies of my *'Speaking for Success'* and *'In the Company of Leaders'* which we re-released to honor TI's 90th. I'll be traveling to Calgary and the D42 conference this Friday for the evening. They asked as many of us Past District Governors to attend as possible and I am honored to do so. They also asked me to bring the Toast to the first timers, which I am pleased to do. Until next time.... **live and lead with the 4 H's as your guide**.

**2014: Last week I got a first-hand appreciation** of what our farmers do to keep us fed when I was asked by a farmer friend if I wanted to learn how to drive a combine.

Of course, I said yes and for the next 7 or so hours drove a humungous combine harvesting a wheat field, about 60 acres, before dark.

It was a bit scary at first to be entrusted with this amazingly large and expensive piece of farming machinery. Stan took me around the field once showing me how everything worked and how to empty what we'd cut into the truck. Then he wished me luck and jumped off. Kind of like a pilot does when they move on to solo. I was a bit nervous at first but got more comfortable as the day moved on, even though I 'dug dirt' a few times. The field looks level from the cab, but you can't see the mounds of dirt under the wheat. Then, you shut it down and get out to dig out the header before starting up again. Interesting lesson.

This picture was taken when I got home. I had stopped for gas and the man there had asked if I had been combining – evidently it showed. ☺

**What have you tried that pushed you past your comfort zone this month?**
Say yes and learn something new and gain a new appreciation for something new as well.

**2014: "The fight is won or lost far away from witnesses - behind the lines, in the gym and out there on the road, long before I dance under those lights." Muhammed Ali**

Often the battles or challenges you 'successfully' tackle and overcome are dealt with in the privacy of your mind or when you are far from the public eye. This is where character and determination come together for your defense and building the foundation for your emergence as a success, defeating or overcoming your challenges in life. Keep fighting my friends!

**Darren Hardy**, publisher of **Success Magazine** just shared a quote from Earl Shoaff that resonated with me, **"The major question to ask on the job is not what I am getting here. The major question is what am I becoming here!"**

Darren went on to say, **"Money is disposable. Character and personal development are indispensable." Hmmmm!**

When you are working through a particularly challenging situation or dealing with people who rub you the wrong way; perhaps that is a good time to ask yourself if your character is being polished and what you are becoming through the process.

**What are you 'becoming' as you move forward? How are you enriching your life and the lives of those you touch?**


## 2014: Canadian Women win Gold in overtime 3-2 over the United States

As Irene will tell you, I am not much of a hockey fan. **She is the fan in our family**. I happened to come into the living room when the women were playing the US for the gold in the 3rd period. They were trailing 2-0 with less than 5 minutes remaining on the clock. I remarked it would be great if they could at least score one goal so they wouldn't be blitzed. Tough to see them playing hard and nothing to show for it.

A minute or so later, just ahead of the 3-minute mark that 1st goal happened. I was glad... but then, just a bit into the last minute they scored again to tie the game and force the US into a sudden death overtime. As history shows they fought off the US surge in overtime to win.

**The real lesson here as demonstrated by both teams was, 'PLAY the whole 60 minutes!'** As Irene said, the US moved into a checking mode (defensive) while the Canadians kept playing to score. The faces on the US team showed their disappointment.

They had it won and then those 'Canadians' fought back to tie and to win. They didn't seem to see that winning silver at the Olympic level was also a win and not a loss.

Both teams played well but the Canadians came to play to win and kept after it, despite evidence that they would loose.

How often have you and I stopped playing to win, going into a defensive mode to 'save' our gains or goals? You never know what might happen if you take one more shot, put in that little bit of extra effort. You might even turn around a seemingly impossible situation.

Bravo ladies, you did us proud and you taught me a **Gold Medal** lesson. Keep skating and shooting (and as Red Green might say, "Keep your stick on the ice!")

*PS: The Canadian men's team took the advice to go out there and 'play like girls' and won gold in their game too.*

## 2014: Life is too short!

I often stop to take pictures of unique, thought provoking, or simply funny sayings as I travel the world.

This one says, **"Life is too short for bad coffee."**

**Isn't that the truth!** I enjoy my coffee and try it as I travel. At times, it is amazing like the Blue Mountain coffee I had in Kyoto, Japan. At times it is ok, but not worth writing home about. What about what we do in serving our clients and audiences?

**Is it worth writing home about?**

*"The will to win, the desire to succeed, the urge to reach your full potential… these are the keys that will unlock the door to personal excellence."* **Confucius**

# 2015

## 2015: Communication is really a part of the 'sales' process

People buy or say *'yes'* to something, for emotional reasons in relation to benefits perceived and sometimes received. They use facts to back up or justify their purchase or decision to get involved. In your communication with people, it would be wise to keep in mind that people will react *'emotionally'* to what you say or write. You are *'selling'* your ideas, your position, your services, your products, and most importantly yourself when you communicate.

Perhaps it would be beneficial to take a moment and discuss the basic reasons we've found that people buy or say 'yes' to something. These emotional needs underlie the reason they buy into your programs, buy your products, or buy you as a person to work with or deal with; why they can be persuaded to say 'yes' to something.

Psychologist **Abraham Maslow** did exhaustive research and concluded that all people had a hierarchy of needs. He ranked them from the most basic to the loftiest: physiological (sheer survival), security, social, self-esteem, and self-actualization. There is one more: transcendence which is all about helping people grow and become better. (works for me)

In **'Secrets of EFFECTIVE Customer Service' Business Enhancing Sales Success** program, I cover the top ten as they relate to giving people more reasons to engage you, trust you, or buy from your company. I have included all 25 here for your consideration (and there are undoubtedly more not catalogued here). In my **'Thinking Beyond the FIRST Sale'** (we explore 51 reasons…)

These can be helpful in your interpersonal skills and dealings with family, friends, employees, managers, co-workers, clients, and suppliers as well. Remember when you communicate effectively, people want to be involved in your life and in helping you succeed. If you want to be successful in leadership, sales, your career, or in your community it would be wise to learn and apply these lessons.

**Emotional needs:**

1. To make money
2. To save money
3. To save time
4. To avoid effort
5. To gain comfort

6.  To improve health
7.  To escape pain
8.  To be popular
9.  To attract a partner
10. To gain praise
11. To conserve our possessions
12. To increase our enjoyment
13. To satisfy curiosity
14. To protect our family
15. To be in style
16. To satisfy an appetite
17. To emulate others
18. To have beautiful things
19. To avoid criticism
20. To avoid trouble
21. To take advantage of opportunities
22. To be individual and unique
23. To protect our reputation
24. To gain control over aspects of our lives
25. To be safe

Whether you are talking one-on-one, presenting to a group of people, or communicating in writing, your audience or readers will be *evaluating* and *reacting* to your words and *'filtering'* them through one or more of the above emotional needs.

**Tough sell isn't it?** But if you have done your homework and know a little bit about the needs, background, and thought processes of those you want to reach, it will be much easier. You can enhance your chances of success by carefully crafting your communication to touch or draw on the emotional needs of your audience or readership. But be cautious in its use. Some would ask, isn't this manipulation? My gut reaction would be to say no! On the surface it might appear that way, but only you know your *'true'* motives.

If your *'true'* motive is to communicate more clearly and more effectively and your desire is to serve them by giving them all the information they need in a way that makes it easier for them to relate to it – then I say go for it!

Having an honest desire to help people is what builds a foundation for success in your leadership, sales, career, or business and helps ensure both longevity and success.

**Works for kids too!** We want our kids to grow up healthy and make decisions that will be good for their future. We need to find ways to appeal to them at their level. This even applies to working with family and friends, as well as clients, co-workers, management, and staff. Wow!

So, remember that communication, especially effective communication, is really a process of selling – selling your ideas, your desires, your dreams, and your future. How effective will you be in persuading people to buy in? How successful will you be in inspiring them to help you?


## 2015: Wishing each of you a Merry Christmas, or if you don't celebrate it, a wonderful time with your family and friends.

This can be a very hectic and sometimes emotional time of the year. It is also a time to relax, reflect, and refocus before you start the new year.

I encourage you to enjoy your time with friends and loved ones while letting your mind germinate about what BIG dreams you want to tackle and bring into creation next year.

**Ask yourself a few questions as you enjoy this holiday period.**

- What do I want to commemorate and celebrate from this past year?
- What changes or tweaks do I want to make to my career or life next year?
- What am I very grateful for? Or whom?
- What BIG DREAMS consumed me this year? Where am I in making them real?
- What BIG DREAMS do I have planned for next year?
- What great adventures do I want to make happen next year?
- How do I want to grow and enhance my skills over the next year?
- How can I be of service or assistance to others in the future?

Just a few idea starters to kick start your year. May this next year be an adventure, lived well, with enthusiasm and embraced with gratitude.


*"Optimism is the faith that leaders to achievement. Nothing can be done without hope and confidence."* **Helen Keller**

# 2016

## 2016: Sailing the Seven C's of Effective Writing

I love to sail; I love being out on the water. In 1988, I joined 3 other men for what I thought would be a *leisurely sail* from Honolulu, Hawaii to Kobe, Japan. Along the way we encountered what the Japanese later told us was a 'baby' typhoon.

We were extremely fortunate to survive it. Later we arrived safely in the Kobe/Osaka harbour.

I've often thought that our written words and our efforts to communicate effectively run some of the same gambits, storms, or challenges as we chart our course and focus on a specific harbour or objective.

I've included some ideas here that might help you avoid or navigate some of the storms and hidden obstacles to being effective in your written communication.

**An effective memo, email, or sales letter** is one that gets results. Business correspondence can enhance or alienate relationships. Well written brochures, sales literature, or websites entice people to act and explore opportunities to deal with you and your firm.

Effective writing communicates the message in a way that makes it easier for the reader to relate and react positively to what they (reader) understand. Effective writing is helped or enhanced by 'charting-a-course' to convey your message with impact.

**Here are seven C's as they relate to effective writing:**

1. **Be clear:** have a definite purpose for writing and make sure it is clearly communicated up front. Be bold and connect quickly. In the middle of the typhoon, we needed to be clear on our commands or risk adverse reactions to the sea.

2. **Be complete:** include all the necessary facts and background information to support the message you are communicating. Partial instructions would not work if we were to survive. Our captain had to make sure we saw the complete picture.

3. **Be concise:** keep in mind the reader's knowledge of the subject and their time constraints. Convey the information as quickly and easily as possible. Keeping it concise (or short) was a life saver, more so when you needed to react immediately to a changing sea or wind pattern.

4. **Be creative:** use different formats (vs. straight narrative) to communicate your message. Q & A format, graphics, Idea lists, etc. Sometimes hand signals were needed when the wind and the sea drowned out our ability to hear.

5. **Be considerate:** keep your reader's needs in mind as you write. Ask yourself, 'Why should my reader spend time reading this?' Make it worthwhile for them to do so! We were motivated to survive, to listen, and to act. Keep in mind your audience or reader might not be as receptive.

6. **Be correct:** by checking all your information is accurate and timely. Double-check your spelling, punctuation, and grammar. Proofread it before you send it! At sea, we couldn't afford to make mistakes, our lives depended on it!

7. **Be credible:** strive to present yourself from a position of reliability and competence. Write to reinforce your message and make it more believable. We needed to trust that our captain, with his experience in the US Coast Guard, knew what he was doing and was telling us for our own good.

I'll move away from the nautical comparisons now and leave you to navigate the remainder of this piece.

## Getting results from your writing

We all want to get results from what we write, don't we? But why don't we? Perhaps we miss the point and miss our reader's point too?

- Write from the reader's` point of view. This will help you write more effectively.
- Use simple non-technical terms to make sure you are clear in your meaning.
- Don't use buzzwords or jargon that may confuse or distract your reader.
- Project a positive attitude to draw your reader into your message. Tell them what you can do, not what you cannot. People react better to positive reinforcement.
- Conclude your writing with a 'call to action' or a specific meaningful request.

**Here are a few more letter-writing tips:**

- Craft your opening and concluding statements to create a favourable impression for your intended reader. Write from their perspective.
- Keep your purpose in mind as you craft your letter. What do you want the reader to do, learn, or understand when they have finished reading it?
- Use the technique of asking questions to get and keep the reader involved.
- Where possible, share flattering or sincere compliments with the reader.
- Include and weave the person's name throughout the letter. Make it personal.
- Please – don't bore your reader with unnecessary history. If needed, attach as an appendix, reference piece, or background piece.
- Use lists to help explain or outline information in an easy format for your reader.
- Bullet points can be a very effective tool in helping your reader navigate your written presentation.
- Check all spelling and punctuation. Remember this is a written representation of you and your firm.
- Don't be afraid to use headlines or sub-headlines to break up your letter and allow reader to focus on each section.
- As mentioned previously, avoid technical jargon and terminology.
- Verify all figures and dates – make sure they are current and accurate.
- Write to explain – not complain.
- Include a PS: hint – people will almost always read the PS: even if they don't read the body of the letter.
- Read the letter to yourself, aloud, or perhaps to another person. Ask yourself, or them, what they understand from reading it? If it does not line up with your purpose – go back to edit it until it does!

Often a quick note, memo or email will convey the message more effectively than a letter. An effective memo or email incorporates all of the above in its structure, with a few refinements.

**Constructing a well written memo or email**

- State your purpose early in the memo or email (subject line is effective)
- Clearly state your purpose for writing it!
- Use direct, to the point statements
- Ensure the writing is well organized
- Use an easy-to-read format

**When should you write a memo or email?**

- Don't write a memo or email where you can settle the situation with a quick call or in person. However, if you need to follow up on a meeting or conversation, a memo or email works well.
- Don't write if the situation evokes emotional undertones or could backfire in your face. Talking face-to-face works better, and it is less 'permanent' than a written note. You want to diffuse a situation not light one under it.
- Don't write to brag or show off your latest triumph or accomplishment. This will alienate more than elevate you from those who read it. If the accomplishment is a shared one and can be used to recognize group or individual achievement, by all means, capture it and share it in a memo with those who made it happen. Bragging about other people can work wonders.

Make sure your distribution list is relevant. Send your memo or email only to those who are directly concerned with the issues contained or raised in your message. Be considerate of their time and don't use memos or emails to reinforce or defend your position, or indirectly put down other people in your firm.

Knowing when to write is often as important as what to write. Here are a few thoughts when you want to capture the moment or message in written form for communicating to others.

- Write to update them on progress or bring them incoming news.
- Share only the necessary or relevant news items.
- Present it in a short, concise, direct format
- Make sure you are prepared and organized – before you write it!
- Discuss relevant achievements, deadlines, and milestones
- Keep your audience continuously aware of events and progress – not just in crisis or deadline crunches.
- Keep it personal and keep them interested
- Keep the communication lines open.
- Demonstrate your competency in your writing.

Writing is a very effective tool in the communication process. It has a longer shelf life and should have more effort invested to ensure that the message is clear, concise and conveys in a timely manner. Charting your course will allow you to safely avoid the storms and obstacles and allow you to navigate effectively to the communication you had in mind when you started your journey. Taking the time to **'think before you ink'** will work wonders in your communications efforts.

# 2016: Big shoes to fill

I love visiting my friends and audiences in Holland and have spoken there on numerous occasions. It is a wonderful place to visit, and the people are amazing. At least twice I have stopped to get my picture taken in this large wooden Dutch shoe in one of the squares. Makes me smile as I slip into it and wonder whose 'shoes' I am big enough to fill as I move forward. Don't be afraid to dream big or to tackle large, seemingly impossible tasks. If you don't try, you'll never have the chance to surprise yourself and amaze your family. **Go for it!**

**I raise a glass to each of you** as you work your way through this collection of writings and ponderings. Over the years I have encountered some amazing people who have added zest, smiles, tears, and love in my life.

**To each of you, I say thanks!** You have enriched my life, and this little book is my gift, in part, to say thanks for everything you've done for me as I journeyed around the globe. It can be a challenge being a speaker, trainer, and author at times. It is so much more fun when we have amazing people, like you, to share it with.

# 2017

## 2017: Phoenix – kindle shorts

I have been a member of the **NSA Arizona** chapter for many years, even though I live here in Canada. I get there once-in-awhile to connect with colleagues and to continue my learning. When I told them I was coming down, I was asked to be a part of the program and share a few tips.

One of the other presenters told me about what he had been doing with kindle shorts in his business mix. **Kindle shorts** are exactly that, short kindle-based e-books that people download and read. Amazon has a service where for a monthly fee you can download as many books as you want. Bob told me that when people do that and read 10% or more, he gets paid. Wow! That motivated me to come home and start creating my own series of kindle shorts. To date we have 8 of them and more to come over the next few years.

Please visit **www.successpublications.ca** for more information.


## 2017: So, you have a problem… that's great!

So, you have a problem, that's great! Are you crazy? Actually…NO!  Someone once told me, **"I'd get paid or determine my value, by my ability to solve problems."**

**If it was easy, everyone would be doing it**, and the competition would be intense. As most customers will tell you, most businesses are not in the problem-solving field. Sad!

**Your ability to solve your client's problems will be directly related to the number of sales and continued growth of your firm.** This is what is needed if you want to enhance your career and move your company and its leadership to the next level creatively and profitably.

The more successfully and **creatively you solve these problems,** the more referrals, and fans you'll see. The more productive you are personally in being a *solution-oriented* owner, manager, or employee will dramatically affect your paycheck, profits, and career path.

I've developed and applied a **simple 4-stage process for dealing with problems and conflicts.**

I've shared this with leaders and their teams around the globe and found it works. This is an effective way to deal **creatively** with customer complaints and concerns as well as other areas of your business and life. These ideas will work with creative and strategic planning, conflict resolution, or in everyday problem solving.

Many of my clients and audiences have a *creative* need to be *productive* in dealing with customers. I've written from that perspective. These steps work in idea generation, brainstorming preparation, and in dealing with company expansion and career enhancement issues just as well. (*excerpted from,* ***"Make ME Feel Special – Idea-rich customer service strategies***) *available from* **www.SuccessPublications.ca**

## Here are the four stages:
- **Invest time in making sure you fully UNDERSTAND the problem.**
- **The key to understanding is to IDENTIFY the real cause.**
- **Take time to fully explore and DISCUSS all the possible solutions.**
- **Act to SOLVE or fully resolve the problem.**

**"The Secret to Effective Customer Service"** or business development is to go through this process systematically and profitably with your clients.

After the problem/conflict has been successfully resolved, **go the extra mile**. By that I mean, doing something *unexpected* to assist the client or to show them you appreciate the opportunity to prove your commitment to their wellbeing. This will help turn an angry or frustrated client into a fan, or better yet… a champion for you and your business.

**Stage One – Understanding the problem/conflict:**

Often a problem/conflict is in a perception of a *difference* of what we expected to happen and what really happened. Here are **three action steps** to help.

**Gather ALL the facts**. Be thorough and investigate. Let the client talk!

**Listen carefully**, and don't be defensive. Wait until they've finished talking and ask more questions to draw them out, to find out their REAL concerns. Why not purchase **Learn to Listen** from www.SuccessPublications.ca)

**Rephrase or repeat** the problem/conflict back to the client to make sure you've heard it correctly and understand what needs to be resolved. Agree on this stage. It's important at this stage to make sure you don't fall into the trap of denying or trying to avoid the problem/conflict. Or worse yet, blaming or attacking someone else, or demonstrating the same negative emotions in response to a customer's complaint. **Just listen, pause, and get the facts!**

**Stage Two – Identify the Real Cause of the Problem:**

You might ask yourself or your client a few *probing* questions to find out what may have caused the problem.

**What has happened?** Listen and ask questions. True assessment of current situation.

**What should have happened?** Ask questions and listen carefully. Was perception a problem? Was it an un-met expectation?

**What went wrong?** This is where you start partnering with the client.

Keep in mind the true cost of an unhappy client. (*Hint: average cost is 8-16 customers lost for each un-satisfied customer.*)

What future purchases could you expect from this client? What future business this client could influence? What the problem at hand costs to rectify?

From research and years of experience, I've noticed that problems/conflicts generally often fall into **four major areas**:

**Mechanics or Function** – product or service failed to work as expected.

**Assembly or use** – someone didn't use it correctly or put it together incorrectly.

**The People Factor** – we make mistakes in how we do something or how we deal with a client.

**Client EGO** – how this PROBLEM makes them look (good or bad) in their eyes and the eyes of their friends and families.

**Stage Three – Explore and DISCUSS possible solutions.**

This is possibly the most critical part in the client satisfaction/problem solving process. We need to fully focus and objectively look at the challenge we've partnered with the client to solve. Here again – a few **simple action steps**.

**Suggest options.** Take time to explore ALL the options that might effectively help solve this problem or at least minimize the impact.

**Ask your customer for their ideas.** Very often, they have a solution in mind, or have some good input that will help you mutually resolve it to their satisfaction.

If they are a partner in the decision, they will help make it work and will be more inclined to be happier with the results. **Their satisfaction will result in referrals for you!**

**Agree on the best solution** or course of action. After you've fully explored the options, make sure you both agree on what and when you will do to resolve it. THEN DO IT!

**Stage Four – Take ACTION to resolve the problem or conflict.**

This is the ***completion stage*** that builds a foundation for a potential long-term relationship with your *formerly* dissatisfied client. Make this a priority focus for your firm.

Once you've agreed on what needs to be done, move heaven and earth to do it, and do it better and quicker than you've promised. Remember, they are watching to make sure you were serious about making them happy. This is your chance to prove your commitment.

Again, **three action steps.**

Physically remove the cause of the problem or take steps to retrain if problem was personnel based. Take corrective action to substitute, replace or repair the product or service. Ask the client if they are satisfied with the changes and action you've taken.

**Going the extra mile.** This is where you cement the relationship by doing something extra, something totally unexpected by the client.

Show them you care and are *genuinely* concerned about the *perceived* inconvenience they've experienced. **Apply your creativity to cementing the relationship!**

One note: **Use your complaints as a creative source of product or service development.**

Each one is an opportunity for you to learn how to better serve your clients, refine your service, or improve your product in the marketplace. This is also an opportunity to expand your business or service by using these creative solutions as stepping-stones, or business building blocks.

**Yesterday's problems are today's new and improved products or services.**

Want to be a creativity leader? YES! Then learn from each lesson your clients give you.

This is an opportunity for you to build a strong foundation for success well into the next decade. **Don't miss the lesson. It might be a "v-e-r-y" valuable one!**

*"Peace is not the absence of conflict but the presence of creative alternatives for responding to conflict – alternatives to passive or aggressive responses, alternatives to violence."* **Dorothy Thompson**

## 2017: Scotland

*Bob at Urquhart Castle near Inverness*

Irene and I toured Scotland for a week and discovered we loved it on so many levels. I had the opportunity to share some ideas with my fellow speakers at PSA-Scotland in Edinburgh. I was pleased to share some ideas to assist them in their quest as speakers and to build their respective speaking businesses. Some great friends!

In addition, I did a program for D71 Toastmasters in Glasgow. I love doing things like this for my colleagues and fellow Toastmasters as I travel the world.

## 2017: Ireland

We spent a week driving around Ireland as well as Northern Ireland. Wow, what an amazing country. Along the way I got the opportunity to speak for D71 in Dublin and Belfast as well as PSA-Ireland in Dublin.

Here is the link to my full-length program for PSA-Ireland:
**https://youtu.be/BA-sd_P96Jg**

We were amazed at how green this country is and how warm and hospitable the people we met were… they made us feel so welcome. We will go back to both Ireland and Scotland when the opportunity arises.

*"Your work is going to fill a large part of your life, and the only way to be truly satisfied is to do what you believe is great work. And the only way to do great work is to love what you do. If you haven't found it yet, keep looking. Don't settle! As with all matters of the heart, you'll know when you find it."* **Steve Jobs**

# 2018

## 2018: Cuba and Dominican Republic

Irene and I love our visits to Cuba and each one has brought home different memories based on the amazing people we meet and the unique places we visit.

This picture is in the favorite bar where **Ernest Hemmingway** hung out when he was in Havana.

We visited Punta Cana in the Dominican Republic for Irene's birthday. The folks at the resort spoiled her rotten, and I loved it.

## 2018: Break Out-of-the-Box Thinking

This will jog your problem-solving skills. You can create novel ideas by **NOT** following expectations, rules, regulations, assumptions, or long-standing traditions, company history or policy. Go against the grain and the status quo to find the ultimate solution you need.

Just for a moment, **remove the '*speed limits*' from your mind** and challenge your traditional linear thinking. Ask yourself a few *strategic* questions to trigger your creative juices.

Look at your problem or idea and ask yourself some questions. This will allow you to change the way you look at them. **A slight change in *perspective* can productively change your results.**

**Take a moment and ask yourself:**
- What if?
- If only?
- Why not?
- Who says?

- Does it apply to me?
- By whose standards?
- Is there another way?

**Continue asking yourself:**

Let's pretend for a minute we had *all* the resources, personnel, and time?
- Is there a second *'right'* answer?
- What happens if I do nothing?
- What is the best that can happen?
- What is the worst that can happen?
- How can I benefit or learn from this experience?

Just a few mind joggers to help kick start your thinking process. Take a few minutes and write some answers that relate to your goal or problem at hand. Your answers should be based or relate to the earlier statements.

## 2018: District tours – as Region 4 Advisor

The District tours were the most exhausting, yet interesting, part of my 15 months as **Region 4 Advisor** for **Toastmasters International.** Each of 14 international regions have advisors whose role is to guide, train, and sometimes be a shoulder to cry on. Because I have my own company, I was able to invest a bit more on each visit instead of just a couple of days in each District. I was leverage well with potential club visits (corporations and other locations), training District leaders, visiting struggling Toastmasters Clubs, and speaking at Toastmasters Leadership Institutes and special meetings. I would come home tired but satisfied that I had help my leaders and their teams give better service and education to their members and clubs.

## 2018: China and Australia

We had the privilege of spending close to a month in Australia visiting with Irene's daughter Amanda and her husband Michael. They live 4 hours north of Perth in Geraldton. We also did some visiting around South Western Australia. We brought back some wine and chocolates for our winter here in Alberta. We stopped over in Hong Kong to break the trip on the way over and again for a short visit (3 days) on our way home. We even took a highspeed train into mainland China where we met a TM friend, **Derek Wong**, who convinced me to eat frogs' legs!

# 2019

## 2019: Barcelona and Rome

We flew into Barcelona at the end of March to spend a few days before we embarked on our 10-day cruise down to Rome. As I do wherever I can, I reached out to the local Toastmasters in that area with an offer to do a program on presentation skills. They said yes and started promoting it. About a week out they contacted me to let me know they were moving it to another location as they had sold out the original one.

We ended up with close to 80 people coming out to learn how to present like a pro. It was an amazing evening. A group of us went for a bite afterwards and sat outside enjoying the pleasure of our company and sharing stories. **I can hardly wait to go back.**

One highlight was meeting two people from **PSA Spain** who were just getting started. In fact, **Ian Gibbs** and **Sara Tendero** booked the same facility for their kick-off meeting in May. In Barcelona, we toured the Sagrada Familia basilica designed by Gaudi which blew my mind. We also wandered the streets, a lot.

They are now going strong. I joined them and am a proud charter member. I will be going back to Barcelona (April 2020) to help them host their very first conference. I'll recruit a few other professional speakers to come over. It will so much fun.

Our 10-day cruise from Barcelona wandered down to Rome stopping at some amazing locations along the way. Croatia, Monte Carlo, French Riviera, Montenegro, Pompeii, Sicily,

We spent 4 days in Rome playing tourist and seeing ancient Rome before flying home. We visited the Forum, Palatine Hills, St. Peters, Pantheon, Sistine Chapel and more. Wow!

We had a guided tour of the Vatican (we met our guide at 7 am) outside the immense doors and she took 4 of us through. Wow, awe inspiring. I dropped off a signed copy of my leadership book and a note for **Pope Francis**. I got a nice thank you note from him after I got home. Surprisingly, it got to him. I was so amazed. Not sure if he read it, but he saw it and said thanks.

One of the tasty highlights of Rome was the **gelato!** It was so amazing. We had it almost every day as there were little stores everywhere. Made with fresh fruit and rich cream, it was a treat to fully savor!

Our last day in Rome, we had two separate helpings of gelato. We stopped in a little place just down from where we were staying (not far from the Vatican) for one in the afternoon. After dinner, we decided to go back for another. We had attempted to chat to the two ladies working there. When we came in for the 2nd time they wouldn't let us pay and the one lady (*pictured here*) came out from behind the counter to give me a big hug. Funny how people respond when you simply make the effort to connect and communicate.

## 2019: Paris, again

**Irene and I love Paris**. Our first trip together was following my presenting in Mumbai. I had a choice of 3 cities for stopovers on the way home. I invited her to meet me, and she chose Paris. I met her at the airport, and we explored.

I spoke at the AFCP (French Speakers Assoc.) in 2015 and was invited back for May to present at the European Speakers Summit which was hosted by AFCP. We now have 15 professional associations in the Global Speakers Federation, I have spoken in 8.

**https://youtu.be/PlVe9d73Uww** follow this link to see an excerpt from my presentation.

We went to see our friend **Mona Lisa** again, took a couple of riverboat rides, and I finally got to visit D' Orsay Museum. We also saw the burned-out Notre Dame, already being cleaned up and readied for renovation. So glad!

## 2019: Take advantage of opportunities

I penned this several years back, but it is still valid as we approach 2020. Business success at its basic essence is based on innovation, solving problems, or fulfilling the needs, wants and desires of our clients.

**Here's a potpourri sampler** of how to take advantage of opportunities to expand or unlock your business potential.

- What business are you REALLY in? Keep asking this question and keep adapting your business to keep it fresh. Hint: think in terms of customer benefits. What do your customers get when they deal with you? What do they really want?

- Combine two or more products or services to create a new one. Perhaps you can work with a strategic partner or ally to develop a new service or product that will bring mutual benefit?

- Take an idea from another industry and transfer it or adapt to suit yours and the needs of your clients. (For example: loyalty cards, air miles/coffee cards/buy 10 get one free promotion.)

- Try something that didn't work the FIRST time. It might now, with changes in technology, resources, client needs, and attitudes.

- Take advantage of the trends or changing interest in the marketplace. This is where your customer service focus will help, a lot!

- Use a different material or process to do a traditional job.  Creativity counts!

- Look for ways to be a value-added company or person, focusing on real customer service. How can you personally make changes to what you bring to your work?

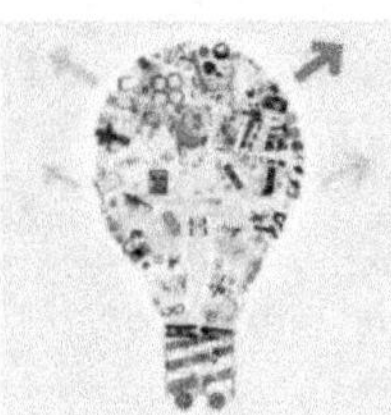

Being creative is often as simple as being willing to risk by trying new or unfamiliar things and activities. Creativity is what solves your problems and builds your long-term business.  Looking at your business with fresh eyes, and from different perspectives is one secret in tapping your inner genius and accessing your Creative S.O.U.L.

## 2019: Planning for a return visit to speak in Barcelona for PSA Spain

As mentioned earlier, I had the privilege of becoming a charter member of **PSA Spain**. They are growing and now have two chapters: Barcelona and Madrid (just starting). I told them I wanted to come back for a visit and speak for them. I shared an idea of turning my visit into a mini conference and inviting some other speaker friends from around the globe to fly in and help us. I will be speaking on April 18, 2020 which is my birthday.

*So, I guess I am throwing an international birthday party.* 😊 *How cool is that! I love my career and the people I get to share it with...*

**Irene and I enjoy cruising.** We did two of them this year. 1) 11-day cruise from New Orleans in the Caribbean and 2) 10-day one from Barcelona to Rome. As you may know, I proposed to Irene on a cruise from Vancouver to Los Angeles, and she said yes! This picture was on the one through the Caribbean. We love taking pictures of us as we travel to help capture the moment and visually remember our good times.

# 2019: I found my lost family

I was adopted about 3 weeks after I was born by two amazing people who became my parents, loved me, and raised me and gave me a sense of value.

I wondered about the young girl (17) who wisely gave me up for adoption when she realized she was too young to keep me when her family was already too large for the small house where they lived. Earlier in the year Irene gave me a 23 and Me kit and I sent it in. Much later she shared an email with instructions, "You need to call this lady, I think she is your cousin."

*Elsie (Jorginson) Sing — my birth mother shortly before her death*

She was… **Susan Dennis** is one of about 45 1st cousins and she organized a quick gathering in Calgary with my 3 adopted stepbrothers, two of three living aunts **Suzie** and **Shirley**, her sister **Sandy**, and several other cousins. *Pictured here…*

My two aunts recognized my birth mom in my face and welcomed me back into the family immediately. Hugs all around. I almost cried!

*Elsie's sons: Tommie, Warren, Bob and Jackie*

I was enthralled as I heard story after story about my birth mom, **Elsie (Jorginson) Sing**, her husband Jack and 4 adopted children. One adopted sister, Rhonda, passed away a while back. It was interesting to meet my 3 adopted stepbrothers, a bit rough around the edges, but it was fun to finally meet them.

I look forward to additional gatherings and to learning more about my birth family and my extended cousins as we move forward.

## 2019: Denver, CO… Toastmasters Hall of Fame induction

### What a ride! My life as Region 4 Advisor

It started with a question from our Toastmasters CEO **Dan Rex**, **"Bob, have you ever considered becoming a Region Advisor?"** My response, **"No, what is it?"**

*Bob at the Hall of fame in Denver*

So began my research into a role that would stretch me by allowing me to work with some of the most amazing leaders across Region 4. I checked into it and the primary role of the Region Advisor is to train, coach, and nudge. "I could do that!", I thought. The process started with a long detailed self-assessment and application followed by several interviews by TI staff and past Region Advisors before a phone call from incoming President, **Lark Doley**. The board had just voted to confirm her appointment of me as 2018-2019 Region 4 Advisor.

Lots of training from TI staff, webinars by current and past Region Advisors and shadowing the current RA brought me to July 1st. I was on my own without a net. ☺ Then the fun began. Prepping for two months to deliver training to our 2018-2019 District Leaders in Chicago, learning my role and occasionally stubbing my toe along the way. And the fun part of playing catch and confirm with our District Leaders to set up and plan my District visits for the fall. They are extremely detailed and need to be pre-approved by TI staff as well as the International President. Whew!

Our time in Chicago started with a full day of rehearsals with fellow RAs, followed by two extremely full days of training and interaction with our new teams. And of course enjoying the convention following our training sessions. Again, Whew!

The best part of my journey was working with my teams across the Region. Coaching, being a shoulder to cry on, an advisor, trainer, and sometimes a nudge as we moved forward into our year together. Prepping for my District visits took on a life of its own as I prepared a series of presentations, training sessions, and getting ready for prospective club visits. Each of my visits was 4 to 5 days. I haven't put this much into my homework since college… perhaps even less there… but it was worth it.

We even did promotional videos to stir up some interest in my forthcoming visit. One entailed me hitch hiking on a busy highway outside of Regina; another with me in Thecla's bathroom with a back up team. This generated quite a few laughs and some discussion and based on the comments during my visit some real interest in attending some of the events where I was speaking. Thanks Lloyd. WE did that for some of my other District visits with similar fun results.

Our international President, **Lark Doley** attended one of my zoom calls with my Region 4 leaders and got them to promise to ***work me hard*** when I came to their districts. **They did!** I was kept busy visiting struggling clubs, doing prospective club visits, corporate visits, speaking with District Executive Council members, Division gatherings, TLI's and even a social outing or two. Along the way we saw some real interest in Toastmasters clubs being formed (followed by action and formation later) some of our struggling clubs get a shot of enthusiasm and move back into active status. Amazing!

*Bob on the road, again!*

I made some amazing friends along the way. We learned together. I shared my ideas with diverse groups across Canada and the USA. Mostly, I got to know our leaders and better understood how I could assist them as we worked through our challenges together.

I hosted monthly zoom calls with various leaders. Some as individual groups, (e.g. CGD, PQD, DD) some with all our Region leaders. I sat in on District Executive Council calls, monthly District Leadership calls and meetings to learn, observe and answer questions along the way. Loved being able to see each person and to encourage them to cross pollinate ideas, share challenges and suggestions to overcome them, and in some cases just vent in a safe environment. I was pleased to facilitate that process as I believe, **"All of us are smarter than one of us!"**

Each month, at 7am MST on the 1st Monday, all 19 Region Advisors around the globe gathered for a call to arms, to discuss challenges, changes, ideas from TI staff and International President, Lark Doley. This kept us focused and energized as we moved into each month. Lark was an amazing leader and would find a way to share ideas and observations to inspire us each month.

*"The challenge of leadership is to be strong, but not rude; be kind, but not weak; be bold, but not a bully; be thoughtful, but not lazy; be humble, but not timid; be proud, but not arrogant; have humor, but without folly."*
**Jim Rohn**

Region 4 met along with our Region 1 leaders in Seattle, mid-January where Region Advisors conducted more training, coaching and individual meetings with our respective teams. Your Region Advisors prepped for a couple of months to conduct the training. Whew!

Starting in April this year we began helping train our successors by doing webinars on various aspects of our roles, allowing them to sit in on our monthly calls and lots of emails and calls to discuss parts of the role, we were finally learning… just in time to pass it off to your new Advisors.

And, **then July 1st we were retired**…

Tired but for the most part fulfilled in dealing with the challenges, growth along the way and with some amazing stories and experiences with our new friends and fellow leaders.

Yes, being a Region Advisor took a lot of work, much more than I had originally expected and allocated for time. However, I grew along side my District Leaders and cherish the memories, the laughs, the shared tears, and the challenges overcome.

In Denver, along with my fellow Region Advisors I was inducted into the Toastmasters Hall of Fame, at the 88th Toastmasters Convention, for my work with you. It was great to see so many of my teams there. I share that honour with you as you were the reason for that journey. Please keep in touch and share your continued success and growth with me.

*"The true mark of a leader is the willingness to stick with a bold course of action — an unconventional business strategy, a unique product - development roadmap, a controversial marketing campaign — even as the rest of the world wonders why you're not marching in step with the status quo. In other words, real leaders are happy to zig while others zag. They understand that in an era of hyper-competition and non-stop disruption, the only way to stand out from the crowd is to stand for something special."* **Bill Taylor**

## 2019: PAPS 2019 Convention in Manila, Philippines

In August I got the opportunity to wing my way to Manila to be a part of the 3rd annual PAPS – Philippine Association of Professional Speakers convention.

What a great experience in this part of the world. The weather cooperated with us. We just missed a typhoon that rolled through two weeks before and another one was scheduled to come shortly after we flew home.

I represented Canada and was one of many international speakers who flew in to participate alongside our PAPS members in this action packed, value-added, one day conference.

The following day I spoke at the 12th annual HR Summit in the same hotel. My friend **Lloyd Luna**, PAPS President and I spoke in Paris. When he went home, he told the organizer that he needed to have me speak at his paid event. Thanks Lloyd!

*Claire Boscq-Scott, Bob, Filipo and Nats Levi in Manila*

Overall, it was an amazing week discovering parts of the Philippines. I had long had this area on my 'to visit' list and finally got the opportunity. I met some amazing speakers from around the globe and had the chance to do some selective sight seeing in Manila and the surrounding area. I can hardly wait to go back.

PS: Claire will be joining us in Barcelona next April for Destiny 2020 (theme).

## 2019: International Speakers Summit

I was asked to be a part of my friend **James Taylor's 3rd International Speakers Summit.** James and I presented in Paris and enjoyed trading stories of travels as speakers. My session was on moving from local to international. I simply shared my journey and he asked me questions on how I made the move and what I had learned along the way. **20,000 people signed up to listen in… wow!**

## 2019: Santa through the years

**Think I have always loved visiting Santa!** *This is me visiting him in Calgary in 1959.*

My folks would take me to meet him and get my picture taken to capture the memory. I got to like it and looked forward to it each year.

When I moved away from home, I stopped doing it for many years. For some reason, I started doing it again and sent the pictures to my mom. It made her smile, and that was worth the trip. I have had my picture taken with him around the world.

After Mom and Dad passed away, I kept visiting Santa and then sent the pictures to my sister and later **Irene Gaudet** when we were dating.

**Now, I do it for me**… and for the enjoyment of being a kid again. I have made friends with my current Santa (Barry White, yes that is his real name!) for 18 years, so far. We have fun together.

*Bob and Santa Barry (White) on one of his 18 visits over the years.*

I often find locations or signs like this and ask Irene to quickly capture the moment. Have you ever wondered if you needed to be **some where**? Or some where else?

That is a great question as we progress in our journey through life. I use my birthday as a time to stop and ponder how I have done in the past year and where (**some where**) I need to be of visit over the next year.

We are booked for Cuba again. For example, in 2020 we are already booked to speak in Barcelona on April 18th with other locations under discussion. Maybe Portugal? Cool!

# About the author

**Bob 'Idea Man' Hooey** is a charismatic, confident leader, corporate trainer, inspiring facilitator, Emcee, prolific author, and award-winning motivational keynote speaker on leadership, creativity, success, business innovation, and enhancing team performance.

Using personal stories drawn from rich experience, he challenges his audiences to engage his **Ideas At Work!** – To act on what they hear, with clear, innovative building-blocks and field-proven success techniques to increase their effectiveness. Bob challenges them to hone specific 'success skills' critical to their personal and professional advancement.

Bob outlines real-life, results-based, innovative ideas personally drawn from 29 plus years of rich leadership experience in retail, construction, small business, entrepreneurship, manufacturing, association, consulting, community service, and commercial management.

Bob's conversational, often humorous, professional, and sometimes-provocative style continues to inspire and challenge his audiences across North America. Bob's motivational, innovative, challenging, and practical **Ideas At Work!** have been successfully applied by thousands of leaders and professionals across the globe. Busy man – productive man!

Bob is a frequent contributor to North American consumer, corporate, association, trade, and on-line publications on leadership, success, employee motivation and training; as well as creativity and innovative problem solving, priority and time management, and effective customer service. He is the inspirational author of 30 plus publications, including several best-selling, print, e-books, reader style e-pubs, and a Pocket Wisdom series.

Visit: **www.SuccessPublications.ca** for more information.

Retired, award winning kitchen designer, **Bob Hooey**, CKD-Emeritus was one of only 75 Canadian designers to earn this prestigious certification by the US based National Kitchen and Bath Association.

In December 2000, Bob was given a special CAPS National Presidential award **"…for his energetic contribution to the advancement of CAPS and his living example of the power of one"** in addition to being elected to the CAPS National Board. He has been recognized by the National Speakers Association and other groups for his leadership contributions.

Bob is a co-founder and a Past President of the CAPS Vancouver Chapter and served as 2012 President of the CAPS Edmonton Chapter. He is a member of the NSA-Arizona Chapter, a charter member of the Canadian Association of Professional Speakers, PSA SPAIN, as well as the Global Speakers Federation. He has retired (December 2013) as a Trustee from the CAPS Foundation. He is also a charter member of PSA SPAIN.

In 1998, Toastmasters International recognized Bob **"…for his professionalism and outstanding achievements in public speaking"**. That August in Palm Desert, California Bob became the 48th speaker in the world to be awarded this prestigious professional level honor as an **Accredited Speaker**. He has been inducted into their Hall of Fame on numerous occasions for his leadership contributions.

Bob has been honoured by the United Nations Association of BC (1993) and received the **CANADA 125 award** (1992) for his ongoing leadership contributions to the community. In 1998, Bob joined 3 other men to sail a 65-foot gaff rigged schooner from Honolulu, Hawaii to Kobe, Japan, barely surviving a 'baby' typhoon enroute.

**In November 2011 Bob was awarded the Spirit of CAPS** at their annual convention, becoming the 11th speaker to earn this prestigious CAPS National award. Visit: **www.ideaman.net/SoC.htm**

Bob loves to travel, and his speaking and writing have allowed him to visit 46 countries so far. Perhaps your organization would like to bring Bob in to share a few ideas with your leaders and teams around the globe.

Visit: **www.HaveMouthWillTravel.com** for more information.

*"My mission in life is not merely to survive, but to thrive; and to do so with some passion, some compassion, some humour, and some style."* **Maya Angelou**

# Copyright and license notes

**The saga continues… 2010- 2019 - A Tip of the Hat collection**

**Bob 'Idea Man' Hooey,** Accredited Speaker, Spirit of CAPS recipient
Prolific author of 30 plus business, leadership, and career success publications.
**www.ideaman.net**



**Photos of Bob: Bonnie-Jean McAllister, www.elantraphotography.com**
**Frederic Belot, www.fredericbelot.fr/fr**
**Dov Friedman, www.photographybyDov.com**
Additional photos from the collection of Bob Hooey

Editorial, layout and design: **Irene Gaudet**, Vitrak Creative Services (a division of
Creativity Corner Inc), **www.vitrakcreative.com**

**ISBN: 9781998014163 IS**

**Success Publications, a division of Creativity Corner Inc.**
Box 10, Egremont, Alberta T0A 0Z0
**www.successpublications.ca**
Creative office: 1-780-736-0009

**Life is fun** and we have lots of opportunities to explore, try new things, meet new people and to make our mark on the world.

This underwater shot was taken on one of our trips to Australia while I was playing with our waterproof camera.

**Have fun my friends!**

# Acknowledgements, credits, and disclaimers

As with each of my books, a very special dedication of this piece of myself, to the two people who meant the most to me, my folks **Ron and Marge Hooey**. Sadly, both my parents left this earthly realm in 1999. I still miss our time together and your encouragement and love. I was blessed with the two of you in my life.

To my inspiring wife and professional proof-reader and publications coach, **Irene Gaudet**, who loves, encourages, and supports me in my quest to continue sharing my **Ideas At Work!** across the world. Thank you seems so inadequate for your timely work in helping make my writing and my client service better! I love the time we spend together!

My thanks to the many people who have encouraged me in my growth as a leader, speaker, and engaging trainer in each area of expertise including *Hosting a successful meeting, training session or conference.*

To my colleagues and friends in the National Speakers Association **(NSA)**, the Canadian Association of Professional Speakers **(CAPS)**, and the Global Speakers Federation **(GSF)** who continually challenge me to strive for success and increased excellence.

To my many **Toastmasters** friends and family around the world, to whom I owe an un-payable debt of gratitude for your investment, encouragement, time, and support when I was just starting down this path; and oh, so rough around the edges.

**To my great audiences, fellow leaders, students, coaching clients, and readers across the globe** who share their experiences and enjoyment of my work. Your positive and supportive feedback encourages me to keep working on additional programs and success publications like this updated version.
My experience with you creates the foundation for additional real-life experiences I can take from the stage to the page, the classroom to the boardroom.

My thanks to a *select* few friends for your ongoing support and 'constructive' abuse. You know who you are. ☺

*Bob keynoting the 2015 AFCP convention in Paris, France. He keynoted the European Speakers Summit in Paris hosted by AFCP in 2019.*

In 2019, he spoke in Barcelona, Rome, Paris and Manila in addition to presenting closer to home. He'd love to come to your part of the world and challenge you audiences and team members to see his Ideas At Work!

In 2020 he is already booked for Barcelona and awaiting news for Singapore and a return visit to Paris. **Why not bring him to your part of the world!**

**Bob 'Idea Man' Hooey**
**www.ideaman.net**
**www.bobhooey.training**
**bhooey@mcsnet.ca**

*"Would you like me to give you a formula for success? It's quite simple, really: Double your rate of failure. You are thinking of failure as the enemy of success. But it isn't at all. You can be discouraged by failure or you can learn from it, so go ahead and make mistakes. Make all you can. Because remember that's where you will find success."* **Thomas J. Watson**

# Disclaimer

**One of the highlights of 2019** was finding and meeting my two aunts **Suzie** and **Shirley** in Calgary. My aunt **Linda** lives out east so will meet her along the way. All my adopted parent's siblings are gone so had thought I had no family left other than my sister and a few cousins. This year I discovered my long-lost family, and I am truly blessed. 3 aunts, 3 brothers and 45 1st cousins.

# What they say about Bob 'Idea Man' Hooey

As I travel across North America, and around the globe, sharing my **Ideas At Work!** I am fortunate to get feedback and comments from my audiences and colleagues. These comments come from people who have been touched, challenged, or simply enjoyed themselves in one of my sessions or one of our publications. **I'd love to come and share some ideas with your organization.**

*"I've known Bob for several years and follow his activities in business with interest. I originally met Bob when he spoke for a Rotary Leadership Institute and got to know him better when he came to Vladivostok, Russia to speak to our leadership.* **When you spoke, I thought you were one of us because you talked about our challenges just like yours.** *You could understand the others, which makes you a great speaker!"* **Andrey Konyushok,** *Rotary International District 2225 Governor 2012-2013, far eastern Russia*

*"I still get comments from people about your presentation.* **Only a few speakers have left an impression that lasts that long.** *You hit a spot with the tourism people."* **Janet Bell,** *Yukon Economic Forums*

*"We greatly appreciate* **the energy and effort you put into researching and adapting your keynote to make it more meaningful to our member councils.** *Early feedback from our delegates indicates that this year's convention was one of our most successful events yet, and we thank you for your contribution to this success."* **Larry Goodhope,** *Executive Director Alberta Association of Municipal Districts and Counties*

*"Thank you Bob; it is* **always a pleasure to see a true professional at work.** *You have made the name 'Speaker' stand out as a truism - someone who encourages people to examine their lives and make adjustments. The personal stories you shared with your audience made such a great impression on everyone.* **The comments indicated you hit people right where it is important - in their hearts.** *Each of those in your audience took away a new feeling of personal success and encouragement."* **Sherry Knight,** *Dimension Eleven Human Resources and Communications*

*"Bob is one of those rare individuals who knows how to tackle obstacles in life to reach his dreams. He takes each as a learning* **experience and stretches for more.** *His compassion and genuine interest in others, make him an exceptional coach."* **Cindy Kindret,** *Training Manager, Silk FM Radio*

"Without doubt, **I have gained immeasurable self-assurance.** Bob, your patience and your encouragement has been much appreciated. **I strongly recommend your course to anyone looking for self-improvement and professional development.**" **Jeannie Mura**, Human Resources Chevron Canada

"I am pleased to recommend Bob 'Idea Man' Hooey to any organization looking for a charismatic, confident speaker and seminar leader. I have seen Bob in action on several occasions, and he is ALWAYS on! Bob has the ability to grab his audience's attention and keep it. Quite simply, **if Bob is involved - your program or seminar is guaranteed to succeed.**" **Maurice Laving**, Coordinator Training and Development, London Drugs

"I have found **Bob's attention to detail** and his ability to fine tune his seminars to match the time frame and needs of the audience to be a valuable asset to our educational program." **Patsy Schell**, Executive Director Surrey Chamber of Commerce

"Great seeing you in Cancun and congratulations on a job well done. **The seminar was a great success! Your humorous and conversational style was a tremendous asset.** It is my sincere hope that we can be associated again at future seminars." **Donald MacPherson**, Attorney At Law, Phoenix, Arizona

**"What a great conference.** It was a great pleasure meeting with you at the Ritz Carlton, Cancun and I shall look forward to hopefully welcoming you and your family in Dublin, Ireland someday." **A. Paul Ryan**, Petronva Corporation, Dublin, Ireland

"Congratulations on the **Spirit of CAPS Award.** You have worked long and hard on behalf of CAPS …**helped many speakers including me** and richly deserve this award. Well done my friend." **Peter Legge**, **CSP, Hof, CPAE**

"I had the pleasure of hearing and watching Bob Hooey deliver a keynote speech several years ago when he gave a presentation at a Toastmasters International Convention. **Bob impressed me greatly with his professionalism, energy, and ability to connect with his audience while giving them value.** I heartily recommend this talented speaker and 'Idea Man' to all who want to move to the next level." **Dr. Dilip Abayasekara**, **DTM, Accredited Speaker,** Past President, Toastmasters International

"I attended **Speaking for Success** in Edmonton. **The mark of a true leader is someone who will lay down their own pride to teach all they know to their potential successors.** To be taught by a man of his caliber was an honor whether you're a beginner like myself or a professional; the experience is well worth it! To Bob - it truly was an honor to meet you. Stay humble and enjoy the great success." **Samantha McLeod**

# Bob's B.E.S.T. publications

Bob is a *prolific* author who has been capturing and sharing his wisdom and experience in print and electronic formats for the past fifteen plus years.

In addition to the following publications, several of them best sellers, he has written for consumer, corporate, professional associations, trade, and on-line publications.

He has been engaged to write and assist on publications by other best-selling writers and successful companies. His publications are listed to give you an idea of the scope and topics he writes about. Bob's **B**usiness **E**nhancement **S**uccess **T**ools.

## Leadership, business, and career development series

- **Running TOO Fast** (8th edition 2022)
- **Legacy of Leadership** (6th edition 2024)
- **Make ME Feel Special!** (6th edition 2022)
- **Why Didn't I 'THINK' of That?** (5th edition 2022)
- **Speaking for Success!** (10th edition 2023)
- **THINK Beyond the First Sale** (3rd edition 2022)
- **Prepare Yourself to Win!** (3rd edition 2017)
- **The early years… 1998-2009 – A Tip of the Hat collection** (2023)
- **The saga continues… 2010-2019 - A Tip of the Hat collection** (2023)

## Bob's Mini-book success series

- **The Courage to Lead!** (4th edition 2024)
- **Creative Conflict** (3rd edition 2024)
- **Get to YES!** (4th edition 2023)
- **THINK Before You Ink!** (3rd edition 24
- **Running to Win!** (2nd edition 2024)
- **Generate More Sales** (5th edition 2023)
- **Unleash your Business Potential** (3rd edition 2024)
- **Maximize Meetings** (new for 2024)
- **Learn to Listen** (2nd edition 2017)

- **Creativity Counts!** (updated 2024)
- **Create Your Future!** (3rd edition 2024)

## Bob's Pocket Wisdom series

- **Pocket Wisdom for Speakers** (updated 2022)
- **Pocket Wisdom for Leaders – Power of One!** (updated 2022)
- Additional PW books are coming as ebooks in 2024

## Kindle Shorts (2017-2020) - more to come in 2024

- **SPEAK!**
- **LEAD!**
- **SERVE!**
- **CREATE!**
- **CONFLICT!**
- **TIME!**

## Co-authored books created by Bob

- Quantum Success – 3 volume series (2006)
- **In The Company of Leaders (95th anniversary Edition 2019)**
- Foundational Success (2nd Edition 2013)

**Visit: www.SuccessPublications.ca** for more information on Bob's publications and other success resources.

**A final note as 2019 winds to a close.** Creating this two-book project has been an amazing opportunity to go back over 22 years of living, adventures, friends, family, and of course adventures. It is fun to realize I learned to write and was able to share a few ideas with you as well as audiences around the world. My thanks to all of you.

A Tip of the Hat to everyone who made me smile, think, stretch and grow over the past two decades. You have enriched my life and I am forever indebted to you. I take you with me in my heart as I continue my adventures.

# Thanks for reading The saga continues…
# 2010-2019 – A Tip of the Hat collection

Each time I prepare to step on the stage; each time I sit down to write I am challenged to deliver something that will be of use-it-now value to my audience/reader.

- I ask myself, *"If I was reading this, what value would I be looking for?"*
- As well as, *"Why is this relevant to me, today?"*

These two questions help to keep me focused and clear on my objectives. They help to remind me to dig into my experiences, stories, examples, and research to provide solid information that will be of benefit and help our readers, when they apply it, succeed. That can be an exciting challenge!

I trust we have done that for you in this updated collection of thoughts, tips and ponderings. *'A Tip of the Hat!'* is my attempt to capture and share some of the lessons learned first-hand from observing and working with some tremendously effective leaders, speakers, retailers, service providers, and business owners.

**Bob 'Idea Man' Hooey, 2011 Spirit of CAPS recipient**
www.ideaman.net
www.BobHooey.training
www.HaveMouthWillTravel.com
www.SuccessPublications.ca

**Connect with me on:**
- **Facebook:** www.facebook.com/bob.hooey
- **LinkedIn:** www.linkedin.com/in/canadianideamanbobhooey
- **YouTube:** www.youtube.com/ideamanbob
- **Smashwords:** www.smashwords.com/profile/view/Hooey
- **Follow me on Twitter:** @IdeamanHooey
- **Snail mail:** Box 10, Egremont, Alberta, T0A0Z0, CANADA
- **Amazon:** www.amazon.com/Bob-Idea-Man-Hooey/e/B00FACOHNY

# Engage Bob for your leaders and their teams

*"I have been so excited working with Bob Hooey, as he has given inspiration and motivation to our leadership team members. Both at the Brick Warehouse – Alberta and here at Art Van Furniture – Michigan; with his years of experience in working with business executives and his humorous and delightful packaging of his material, he makes learning with Bob a real joy. But most importantly, anyone who comes in contact with his material is the better for it."*
**Kim Yost**, *retired* CEO Art Van Furniture, *former* CEO The Brick

## Motivate your teams, your employees, and your leaders to 'productively' grow and 'profitably' succeed!

- Protect your conference investment - leverage your training dollars.
- Enhance your professional career and sell more products and services.
- Equip and motivate your leaders and their teams to grow and succeed, 'even' in tough times!
- Leverage your time to enhance your skills, equip your teams, and better serve your clients.
- Leverage your leadership and investment of time to leave a significant legacy within your organization and life!

**Call today** to engage best-selling author, award winning, inspirational leadership keynote speaker, leaders success coach, and employee development trainer, **Bob 'Idea Man' Hooey** and his innovative, audience based, results-focused, **Ideas At Work!** for your next company, convention, leadership, staff, training, or association event. You'll be glad you did!

**Call 1-780-736-0009 to connect with Bob 'Idea Man' Hooey today!**

**Learn more about Bob at: www.ideaman.net**

Visit: **www.SuccessPublications.ca/BusinessSuccess-Tips.html** for special business building success tips, just for you.